New Baltic Poetry

Edited by Jayde Will

New Baltic Poetry

Edited by Jayde Will

PARTHIAN

Supported by the Ministry of Culture for the Republic of Latvia and the Latvian Writers' Union, the Lithuanian Culture Institute and the Cultural Endowment of Estonia.

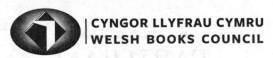

Parthian, Cardigan SA43 1ED
www.parthianbooks.com
First published in 2018
ISBN 9781912109050
Design and layout by Alison Evans
Printed by Pulsio

Contents

Latvia

Estonia

Mats Traat

Introduction

What is new Baltic poetry? For the purposes of this book, it is poetry written by authors from the Baltic largely from the last ten to fifteen years, with a few exceptions made for iconic poems that had not yet been translated into English.

The selection process for choosing the eighteen poets you find before you was guided by a few principles: showcase a mixture of generations, have gender parity, and include those poets that, though they may be well-known in their own country, and are even translated into one or more languages, had yet to have a full collection in English.

Though there have been poetry anthologies that include Baltic authors, or have country-focused volumes in a series, few anthologies have focused on bringing together the three Baltic countries in one book, the most recent being *The Baltic Quintet* (Wolsak and Wynn Publishers, 2008), which also included Sweden and Finland.

Introductions in such anthologies tend to draw on parallels to give shape to the book at hand, however, having witnessed and avidly followed the changes in the Baltic over the last fifteen years, I don't feel in my heart that this would be an honest assessment of the present state of Baltic poetry.

It may come as a shock to readers and those not familiar with Baltic poetry, but I find more differences than similarities in the poetry of the region since the early 1990s when the three Baltic countries regained their independence and started on their paths to new societal vistas. These differences, which are dependent on cultural, economic, and historical circumstances, are too numerous for the scope of this introduction, especially as influences today can come from any part of the world, and it's scarcely possible to keep up with all these factors, even if you take a year-by-year survey of the poetry that is coming out in each country.

But isn't the Baltic region one big cultural monolith? Don't they at least know each other's writers? Unlike the former Yugoslavia or former Czechoslovakia, where intercultural poetic exchange seems to be alive and well, Baltic unity in the sphere of poetry over the last fifteen years has been often lacking, an exception being Baltic poetry festivals and periodicals publishing each other's poets, and a few translators like Latvian poet Guntars Godiņš, who is a well-known translator of Estonian literature, and Lithuanian poet and translator Vladas Braziūnas, who brings Latvian poets into Lithuanian.

Though some authors from the Baltic have achieved prominence abroad (such as Estonian poet and novelist Jaan Kaplinski, and Lithuanian poet and writer Tomas Venclova) most writers have yet to attain greater recognition in the English-speaking world. It is, however, not due to a lack of erudition or poetic sensibility, but rather a lack of their work out in the world. I find this is often due to a shortage of translations, which I hope this book can have a small part in correcting.

Despite my plea to the reader to not see the Baltic region as a whole, I do see the sense and need to present these countries together, precisely because by this, one can see their different character. I am all for a variety of voices and styles, which is needed in every epoch, and never more so than today.

A hearty thanks goes out to the translators: Rimas Uzgiris, for taking on the job of selecting and translating the authors for the Lithuanian section, Ieva Lešinska for taking a lion's share of the translation work for the Latvian section, and Adam Cullen for being gracious with his time during a very busy period, and contributing to the Estonian section. And last but not least, to Alison Evans and everyone at Parthian for entrusting me with the task of putting the book together.

Jayde Will

Lithuania

Translated by Rimas Uzgiris

Marius Burokas is a freelance writer, translator and reviewer for magazines and radio. He is also editor-in-chief of the online magazine, *Vilnius Review*. He made his poetry debut in 1999 and has since published two further collections, winning The Young Yotvingian Prize and Antanas Miškinis Literary Prize. Burokas is a member of the Lithuanian Writers' Union and the Lithuanian Association of Literary Translators.

Being's Dotted Line

Can it be
that I remember
only heat
and nature's blank

for when I emerged
from recurring attacks

of darkness
in a kind of muck

I walked
drank
wrote

finding nothing
to hang on to

while the walls of the city
broke no bones about it

and I didn't even scrape
myself on stone
or lose so much as a finger

I learned quite well
how not to be

groping my way
to the light switch
and
to oblivion's clasp
and
under sheets of twilight

and
over wasted plains

Now, I don't stay
anywhere
for long

I never have time
to tell the story

of how dismally
we all end up

and how happily
we celebrate after

what cannot be coughed up
from my tarry lungs
in this brightly burgeoning
month of August?

the cooling world
withdraws
and seams, joints, cheek-bones
become clear

light
becomes parchment
syrup and subsides

in the evening
there is too little of you

as we sit down together
and watch
the fog slip
from the trenches of hills

silent
like your breath
and our warmth

or like fingers
searching for other fingers

U and J

bumpy backs
dainty mermaid bones

they breathe
like birds
caught in my hands

on both sides
little puffs of breath
they lie awake

and whisper
tell us a story
about the world
about jellyfish
tell us
what electricity is
how trees grow
and why
paper is white

I lie awake
hearing my
deep breaths

the most trustworthy
source of information
the philosopher's stone
an old
encyclopedia

the father
who ruined so much paper
covering

the pit of the past
with the flesh of the future

I speak
to their blank
slates

hoping

I'm right

The Belt

What nourishing
Nostalgia
These Frosted Flakes

Turn back the cold past
And still
It breathes on you

Like the reaper
Who, as we know,
Cuts us down
In our very bloom

Hot and
Cursing

We want to howl
In a scented field
But I go
Where I am sent

Small

Ruffled

My father
Waits for me

Holding Orion's belt
In his hands

Incantation

It had to begin
From blood
Patching itself up out of hopes
Sweet sweat and sighs

It needs to quietly tap out
Its embryonic
Little ABCs

It needs quite a lot
It's curious
And afraid

We move quietly through the furniture
And life
Afraid to scare it off
So cute and so small
So strange

I've stopped cursing

She eats everything

And we

We
By the grace of God
Are not alone

7

From the cycle 'Annotated Photographs'

Fred Herzog, *Man with Bandage*, 1968

he cut himself shaving
and painstakenly pasted
with fingers trembling in fury
a bandaid cross on his chin
then fled as he was
in his white T-shirt

the city is empty
only widows in black
warm themselves in morning sun
while taxi drivers nap
the black widows
trace his passage
and their lips mumble

> sonny
> we heard you last night
> your dreams are dreary
> cratered
> we listened
> to your lungs
> wheeze
> and your heart pound
> we know
> you have life
> as far as your hands reach
> and death
> from head to toe

he stands
stock still

in the bracing air

three streets stretch
before him

and

the yellow light

flashing

flashing

Algimantas Kunčius, *Palm Sunday* by The Gates of Dawn, 1968

outgrown coats
scratched up boots

back bones
like cobblestoned streets

with stinging water
in their eyes
and three tongues
in their mouths

they clutch their willow fronds

- - - - - - - - - - - -

all those years
all those years
have passed

and only the crests in copper coins
have changed

Jan Bułhak, *Evening Prayer*, 1900

to kneel on
the back pew
in aching cold

is there space for me?

alone
under the vault

in you, behind you
under your shell

is there?

- - - - - - - -

maybe I don't need
to ask questions

you already answered
with my life

Benediktas Januševičius

is a poet, prose writer, translator and literary critic. Additionally, he is a photographer and cameraman, calling himself a 'chronicler of Lithuanian literary life'. He has exhibited several collections of visual poetry and has a Lithuanian poetry channel on YouTube. Januševičius's poetry has also been translated into Latvian, Russian, Polish, Belarusian and Portuguese.

we grind the stones one into another
this goes on for hours and hours
then we have our holiday
and we count the autumns
we assemble their coffins
we grind the stones one into another
and watch the smoke rise
this goes on for hours and hours
then we have our holiday and
we vanish or maybe fall asleep
waiting for a fair wind
we count the autumns and we make
coffins
this goes on for hours and hours but
the street's clamour
inhibits our concentration
this goes on for hours and hours
just as the sleeping autumns go on
just as the stones and the wind

, a bar, a bottle, this and that as well,
it seems i'm happy to quietly pass

away, i heard somewhere that it drags
along behind wilted manuscript pages

slipping by – though Cummings spoke
the truth saying no one is really a loser

for all time and yet maybe i'm wrong
maybe i never heard that anywhere

but my errors have an inhuman ache and
this hurt hobbles my soul, according to

Darius it's not proper to use people's
surnames, it's like undressing in public

and wanking, much better to ask someone
(if nobody offers) to spot me two or better yet

three beers and when finally darkness falls,
to recognise the footsteps of death

until those, too, are gone,

Family Scene with a Premonition of Slaughter

rabbits rabbiting
ra bit rara babbit
bit ra rabid ram

bam rabbit ramming
rabid ra bit ram
ba baby rabbits run

rara rabbit bits
of rabid meat bit
rabid rabbiting fox

out foxing bit foxy
outfoxed rabbit
fox bit rabbit run

on symbols

let's talk about symbols
in these symbolic times, the symbol requires special
   attention!
we must look through, count, and newly evaluate all
symbols, regardless of their importance, weight or price

who decided that the lyre is the symbol of poetry?
these days, poetry
could be accurately represented by a DJ stand

who made doves the symbols of love and peace?
maybe doves want to peck and coo but can't – they have to
   symbolise
how did it come about that owls symbolise wisdom, and
   turkeys – foolishness?
because the owl flies away, and we eat the turkey?
who forced the hare to symbolise youth, and the turtle –
   immortality?
maybe the hare is tired of running, and the turtle wants
   some peace?
do they need to symbolise anything? let them crawl along
   in liberty!

a garden of symbols appears tempting
in which almonds ripen and symbolise chastity
cherries bloom in the name of masculinity
the oranges are fragrant of fertility
apples of wisdom ripen
while pears spread health and hope

nothing is lacking, except maybe music
so let's organise an orchestra of symbols!
here's a flute, it'll take care of feelings
and the guitar will fill the soul's emptiness with its beauty
    and majesty
divine drums will pound out heavenly truth
but the harp will calm us down
reminding us that nothing is eternal

so while the orchestra of symbols plays, let's think about
what the crow pooping on our shoulder symbolises – the
    grace of god?
what does the stone promise as it flies at our loved one's
    head? – more stability
finally, what does the mushroom cloud announce? – what
    else but the end of all symbols

in fact, what kinds of lives do symbols live?
how do they carry their heavy symbolic weight?
do they pay taxes?
do they get social security benefits?
do symbols die?
they do die! e.g., the auroch – a very dead symbol
so then who takes care of the funeral?
where is the symbol cemetery?

what is the price of symbolism? what is its meaning?
why do we need words if nothing is said with them?
what use are symbols if people are not worthy?
if they themselves have become symbols?

a million women are sold every year

how much do women cost?
how much does a first-rate second-hand third-world woman
    cost?
how much does a woman cost who knows her own worth?
how much do you have to lay out these days for a woman
    who has cheapened herself?
what amount do you have in mind, saying to a woman,
    'my dear'?

how much does a fresh woman cost? a lightly pickled one?
how much is a smoked woman? boiled?
how much is a well-preserved woman?
how much is a married woman? and divorced?
a woman with many children? and single?
how much is a woman in search of something? and a lost one?
how much is an enlightened woman? and a darkened one?
how much is a bicycle-riding woman? a car-driving
woman? and a woman flying an airplane?
how much is a woman with suicidal tendencies?

which woman is worth more: beautiful or smart?
does a heavy woman cost more than a light one?
is a naked woman cheaper than a woman fully-clothed?
where can you get a hot woman for a cool winter's night?
where do you look for a cold woman on a hot summer's day?

tell me, what should i get: a woman or a book? maybe a stool?
tell me, please, when will a new shipment of women arrive?
could you tell me which women will be fashionable in the
    near future?
will it be black and white women, or technicolor?
how about indifferent women or noble ones? made-up or pale?
imported women or local ones?

varnished women in high frames or carefree crazy women
smelling of cheap booze?

is it worth it to have an artificial woman as opposed to a
    normal one?
can you buy a woman on lease? in parts?
how much is one kilo of woman?

how do you tell contraband women from legal?
what determines the fluctuations in the prices of women?
what discounts are available for women?
who controls the woman market?

where is the closest rental place for women?
who could lend me a woman? just for a little while?
are there any women for free?

who the hell sells women?
and who buys them?

optimistical

a black cat ran across the road?
good thing it wasn't a panther! a panther might have stopped

a bird flew into the window?
imagine what would have happened if it had been a cow

you dreamed a bouquet of chamomile? not so good
but it would be worse to dream a litre of booze

the citizen you were slinking along behind spit three times
over his shoulder and hit you in the face?
just be glad! another would have decked you

you cut your head open?
well, your legs are sound – you can go for a walk

you lost a hundred large?
it's nothing, you could have blown a thousand

your flat was burgled?
you see, they didn't burn it down

someone called you a loser today?
pay no heed. next time, they'll call you an idiot

you were fined?
relax, they could have jailed you

you caught a cold?
good thing it's not cancer

you had a son?
be happy you didn't get twins!

your spouse left you? and so what?
you'll find another. maybe even worse

they tossed you out of your job?
they could have tossed you out of the ninth-floor window

the mayor says you have to ride a bike?
good thing it's not a toboggan
it's hard to slide along bare pavements

the government is collapsing... let it go!
what matters is that no one starts a war

what's that? there's a war on?
not so bad. no one has died, right?

you've been hurt? you're bleeding? dying?
perfect! your sufferings will soon be over!!!

and now, before you close your eyes for eternity
breathe deeply and smile

(another, for the love of god, would have survived)

Kulturarbeider jobber på en bringebæråker[1]

he picks berries as the sun sets
choosing the prettiest
putting the ugly ones aside
throwing out the rotten

his hands are freezing, fingers numb
soaking wet, he barely knows if it's raining or not

labelled an enemy agent in his homeland
an anarchist jober[2]
a loser of a man
author of obscene poetry
stuck in the early 20th century
written about in Lithuanian poems and even mentioned
    in novels
having almost forgotten his name, the man thinks
this may well be the best job he has ever had

in his thoughts, he thanks his friends who took him to this
    wealthy country
he feels safe among the raspberries
no one dupes him here, no one makes him work in vain, no
one plans not to pay
    they don't do things like that here

the cultural worker
bends down and stands up a hundred times a day
disappearing in the raspberry bushes then showing up again
waking bumblebees
he watches clouds fight over the mountain

---

1 Norwegian for 'The cultural worker works in a raspberry field'
2 'jober' is Russian for 'fucker', as well as homonymous with the Norwegian
  'jobber' of the title.

he shakes heavy drops from the fruit
he picks one at a time
two at a time
three at a time, four – five at a time
he collects the big red berries in black boxes
when they fill up he brings up empty ones

the cloak of cloud cracks and a ray of sun breaks through
deer appear in a clearing on the hillside
the Norwegians will probably shoot them within a month
but for now, the northerners enjoy
thick, juicy, fragrant
tantalisingly red raspberries
norske kvalitetsbær – says the advertisement on the
 cardboard box
decorated with drawings of Viking ships

nearby, in the strawberry field, a Polish couple kisses
the cultural worker smiles – good for them, life is now, in
 every moment
never later, not sometime after work is done
the strawberries are on their way out, but the raspberries
 have just begun
the kisses aren't going anywhere

when he finally drags himself home
the cultural worker will not manage to write this text
but before falling asleep, he will manage to warm up and
pop some cherry ice cream in his mouth

on fish

does the sand fish understand the rain fish?
do dark fish sometimes meet sunfish?
does the morning fish follow upon the moon fish?
does the evening fish greet the sunset fish?
and why does the wind fish always vex the candle fish?
yet for the lantern fish the wind is neither here nor there!
does the hope fish never go wrong?
why doesn't the time fish swim against the stream?
are there such fish?

there are all kinds: winged, scaled, toothed, holey,
   cartilaged, bony, knuckle-finned and even double-scented!
so let's continue:
where does the long-fingered fish lead the short-legged fish?
what did the hypocrite fish get up to this time when it got
   away from the honor fish?
does the shepherd fish herd seahorses?
does the sea urchin sleep under the sea fir?
does the custodian fish get along with the pig fish?
will a sprout fish grow from the seed of a fish?
of what does a refrigerator fish dream?
and what does a battery fish want out of life?

as I said, there are many kinds: red, blue, yellow,
   multi-coloured, even uncoloured, and there are invisible
   fish, decorous or insidious fish, educated and barely literate
   fish
thus the fish crayon crumbled by the fish board – maybe the
sea pen could help?...
thus from fish lips slips the word fish
and from the word fish slip fish letters
just fis or fi
fi fi fi without much sense
but after a fish full stop it's wrong to put a fish comma

23

fi fi fi
sh sh sh
free fish clamber through trees
thus from the tree top the fish crow glances in pride
it looks to the skies
it doesn't know what it sees, perhaps graceful fish clouds, or
   maybe some heady fry of birds

as i said, there are all kinds of fish:
butterfly fish frolicking in sea lilies, angel fish fighting with
   devil fish, hatchet fish aiming for the soles, a sea fox, also
   a sea toad
but sometimes it's simply nice to see how on the table fish
flutter boiled fish fried fish
resting fish sausage
or fish cheese
as the plated fish dissolves into jelly fish:
fi fi fi, sh sh sh
until finally finished

Antanas Jonyas is a poet, writer and translator. He worked as an editor at Vaga Publishing House and led the cultural office of the TV channel, Baltic TV. First published in 1973, Jonyas has written numerous poetry collections, poetry for children, satires, critical articles and a play for children. He has won the Gėlė Prize for the best poetry debut, best young author and Lithuanian Writers' Union prize for best book of the year, received the Poetry Spring Laureate award in 2002, and the National State Award of Culture and Art. He is a member of the Lithuanian PEN centre, and of the Lithuanian Writers' Union.

Weatherpain

The winter's day will shake its spleen
rattling like a lumbering machine
sharing the riches of its solitude
with the lonely haunts of childhood

what matter that friends have betrayed us
it is given that friends will betray us
the tinkling coins of February's bright
joy trip into the chest of raw twilight

crackling radios will soon announce
the unneeded accurate hour
in this city even more empty than I
the drug store's closed we can just die

On the Road to Palmyra

Strong enough to remain myself
and yet to melt away like love's ice shelf
a prisoner on a road with no plan
carrying a ragged bundle that bursts
with the un-worked hides of lambs
tortured by hunger and thirst
I carried an insidious burden in mind
of guilt and pain yet afraid to turn back
to see with my own blood-stained eyes
the glorious land of my memory's track

I was waiting hoping for a city to shine
to relieve my eyes burned by dusty wind
for there is a locked reality that rings
in our words when with ineffable sighs
the spirit intercedes for us
and when a gleaming blade collects
the crumbs of poisoned bread from stone
it is ready again to pierce and cut
a meagre opening into a luxurious
land which the Lord has not made my home

I lack the strength to believe
I lack the strength but I believe
but even believing I begin to see
how antefix akroterion palmettes
appear and vanish before my eyes
a stone under my head a knife in my palm
drops of blood on the blade as evidence
where mirages scatter love's covenants

and the years of eternity quickly pass
lying down quietly like cenotaphs
over my naked qualms

The time is up the season's over
they spruce up the graves for All Saints'
Day scrubbing stones the ash has covered
while the aquarium of the city lies vacant

an ozone bubble breaks up in heaven
and scatters scales that rustle from on high
while fireworks bloom in a leaden sky
under the overturned goblet of dawn

illnesses relapse for the worse
and again the exchange of illusions
I step once more into their naive snares

November washes clean its mackintosh
while the white eyes of myriad golden
fish gaze blankly into the turbid air

Blossoming Cherry Trees

In the window's blue frames
a pink peony has bloomed
and poems are like cream
that you lick from a dream

a cherry tree under the window
splashes the sky with flowery crepe
as in the golden-age of Dutch painting
cherry snow splashes over the square
and a woman stretches from her pillow
she closes the chest of her feeling
glancing brazenly at the streetscape
with an ermine's piercing stare

golden dust motes start to dance
in passionate circles by the street
while a spark rises up like a stake
and just then that moment hence

in the garden it begins to seem
that the wattle-fence will not
contain the hoard of blooms
which explodes in a flash of a shot
and in the woman's hand a needle
of bent-grass glass suddenly gleams
veering straight for an unguarded temple
like a bee but painlessly as in a dream

The Traveller's Sorrow

evening covers itself with the stitch
of the sun's quickly setting skirt
and a traveller's staff appears
through musty autumn air

a threshold of crumbling cement
a rotting well-curb cover
the broken crank of a cup

all night he will try to shut his eyes
though he knows it is futile to strive
because someone has already tried:

a) he will depart at dawn having missed
the stars locked up in the well
b) a man on the road will ring his bell
and the stars will die out with a hiss

Sleeping Beauty

Who am I in this room
in this city and this world

your gently vibrating nostrils
your barely opened lips
and the throat's pulsating vein

do I actually still exist
in this bedroom's white concreteness
so easily obliterated
by your immaculate sleep

suspended above your countenance
my contours are fading away
and in a flash I lack a way
to feel the encroaching horror

Room

In this room I find my homeland
because here I fall asleep with you

the keys still hang from the door
the radio station has gone dumb

after playing its polkas and quadrilles

in this room I find my homeland
and here I could even meet my end

you flex just like a shepherd's switch
that drives the herd into the hills

it saddens me when you go out
so I take up this book about

our past – our so often left unspoken

Snowball

Everything melts: time and people
and she with an apple in hand, waiting for the train
the round wheels trundling over junctions
'it is easy to judge, but hard to testify'

someone once said to me and I thought
it's not that my love it's not that at all
if we have something virtuous left in us
because something vicious
comes clattering on this express
in this clean car
in this midsummer train
where dirty snow drips
from the conductor's pocket

she slept on the hard bench
while the apple rolled along the floor
and through the melted snow

Aušra Kaziliūnaitė has degrees in
history and religious studies, and is now a doctoral
student of philosophy at Vilnius University. She has
published four books of poetry and has received
numerous national awards, including the Jurga
Ivanauskaitė Prize and the Young Artist Prize of the
Ministry of Culture.

stuffed

one day, by the dumpster, i saw an abandoned stuffed bird
i saw it and forgot, but it didn't forget me, it even began to
     stalk me—
wherever and whenever i would go, whomever i would
     meet, i saw the ragged bird

at first, i pretended not to see it
let it show itself, what do i care – it neither chirps nor pecks
     at me

but eventually, it grew rude – appearing not only in public
     places—
among students, listeners, pedestrians—
but showing up among friends, perching even on my loved
     ones' heads

so i tried to make nice, asking – what are you doing here
     and what do you want?
but the stuffed thing just squatted there – silent
and my father, on whose head it eventually perched, only
     looked at me enquiringly
dad – i whispered – there's a bird on your head!
but he just waved his hand, you know – big deal

from that time on, i began to see the stuffed creature in my
     dreams—
no escape – i hardly slept, i barely ate, i barely was—
and i would keep seeing it – always frozen in the same pose,
     mute, frayed,
though it began to seem to me that it was smiling – the
     stuffed bird was mocking me

so i finally snatched it up and threw it with all my strength
   at the wall, only, it turned out,
that wasn't the wall, but a mirror.

that was the first time i saw a bird fly
in a mirror

and so what, if god is a seagull

all our history of trying to see, craves not to see

for so long we looked for confirmation
that this time it's for good, that now everything is really real
that to the very grave, etc., etc.

time and time again, we wanted clear and tangible evidence
something concrete and visible
but so what if it's there, and so what if god exists

and so what, if god is a seagull, turning his head to all sides
    in disdain
swallowing fishes live, and shitting on a Belarusian writer

and so what, if god is orange juice
whose expiration date is missing and which
some uncle Stan bought for breakfast some six years ago

and so what, if god is that athletic young man
with brown eyes, showing the exact measure of his penis
on a gay website

and so what, if god is—
only we don't notice him

coltsfoot will grow along the fence

someday, all my friends will die
my relatives and loved ones too
my enemies will die and all my neighbours
the passers-by whom i once met on the street
will vanish from the surface of the earth

my classmates and colleagues
teachers professors co-workers
will die

all the people will breathe their last
with whom i wore
for reasons unknown
the same uniform of time
though i never fought
in any of its battles

birds who once flew
above my head held high
will die and the dogs i used to hear howl
on spine-chilling nights outside the city
will grow silent for all eternity

coltsfoot will still grow along the fence
tired grapes will rest on arbours
but no one will call me by name
and i myself will not be

but then
carefully
head slightly cocked
i'll watch the strange dogs
grapes and coltsfoot
and then

for the first time
i'll really see the flight of birds

and the couple hurrying by
will scroll
their eyes
along the bench
on which i sit

and they will know
that i see
the flight of birds
differently

and that
i am
those things i don't know
the dogs the grapes
and the coltsfoot

horse races

at the camp, people's bodies lie about on horse manure
unmoving, but running
snoring

and they don't die

if they were dead, we would say
how cruel, there were little kids there
they cried for a few minutes after they were shot
and it would be very very sad, and we would look at
  each other
meaningfully, then go to Maxima to buy white bread and
we would watch TV shows, doing everything to forget
  more quickly
we would rearrange our furniture, talk about art
copy out a recipe for cake from a book, talk about art again

but now that they're not dead, lying in the camp, in the
pen,
  enclosed
and surrounded by soldiers, stretched out on racehorse
dung
we hate them more than ourselves, and we do everything to
  forget them
as quickly as possible
we go to Maxima to buy white bread, we watch TV shows

we go to Maxima to buy white bread

alien planet

the computer says – we've arrived
it's generally not very talkative, but has been jabbering
for hours now about the pruning of fruit trees
it says – we have reached our journey's goal

my toes are numb
i climb out of the spaceship
and look around, gathering samples for scientists—
i walk about a room identical to my own
nothing lives for light years all around
there are no curtains
it's quietly snowing outside
garlands glitter in windows across the street
children push and shove on the pavement

nothing but cosmic loneliness and stone

three scenes

spring

sitting next to you I can smell
the scars hidden by your clothes

magnolia blossoms
pushing through your skin

✕✖✕

even when nothing is left
the crumpled sheets will remain
the deep breaths
and your fingers
on the body of summer's end

ice

one more careless step
one more stupid smile
and the ice splits, cracking
now I'm really falling
into you

omelette

i was planning to cook an omelette
i broke one egg
then another
and in the third i found a grimy boy

sitting there, parentless, alone
in a shopping mall
with a small box at his side

i looked around to see if anyone saw
then continued to prepare
breakfast

fortune

in a flash, i am all those people for whom fortune smiled
but they are afraid to smile back
so they look down at their feet and blush

they just look down and blush

even though no one has smiled for some time

in a flash, i am all those people who feel superior to others
and all those people who feel inferior to others
and i am
a snail
a live snail in a North African bazaar

i find myself
in a coiled basket with other snails

slowly unfurling my antennae

tourists pass
taking pictures

Giedrė Kazlauskaitė published her first book of poetry entitled *Songs of Hetaerae* in 2007. She was awarded the Young Yotvingian Prize for best young poet in 2009 and her second book of poetry, *Las Meninas*, was selected as one of the Book of the Year Campaign's top five poetry books of 2014. Her third book of poetry, *Singertraume*, was published in 2016. Giedrė has worked for a number of youth magazines and published essays and reviews in several cultural publications. Since 2010, she has been the editor of the weekly cultural periodical *Šiaurės Atėna*.

Men's Power

I dreamed a woman again,
her head, marinated in formalin,
pulled out of a jar for a portrait.

She was way up high.

I named her Aunt Olympe (de Gouges), caressed
her puffy cheeks, I didn't want
her ever to die.
So much is said about justice
and other legal matters, but I never understood.
Aunt Victoria came along with other
god-fearing aunts to get in our way,
so I rushed her to the guillotine at dawn.

Upon waking, I ran first thing
to the dining room, to bounce on
Uncle Sigmund's leg,

but he broke it dancing the pink flamingo
with a girl from Ipanema.

I went out to the garden, hoping to find the swings,
but the neighbourhood kids were on them already
and wouldn't let me join in.

So, I took my pyjamas off, and then they ran away.

Only Uncle Sigmund dared to come near,
pushing a stroller, holding
Aunt Olympia's head in his hands
like a ball of yarn.

The antique postage stamp
I found – paging through
an old book
in the library—

real women
in pretty clothes
with long, colourful nails.
They turn me on in autumn,
as at the movies, they seem
to be on this side of the screen.

I search for girly jewellery,
pink bracelets to fit your narrow wrists
held poised above the zither.

I will send you a tardy letter,
a few decades before us both,
replete with German postage stamps
from the interwar years.

When the television blares
from the other room – I feel like
I live above an Eastern bazaar.

Let me tell you –
I am not afraid to undress
in front of the cat,
even if he happens to be
someone else's reincarnation.

Such is my solitude.

You gifted me your sketches of frogs,
your musical notes and piglets.
I draw lines around your clefs,
colour their tones,
ones rarely heard,
sung through your nose.

I tend to your farm
locking up the clefs
like a butcher
running late—

strings and colours
quietly hum.

Arranging the shelf, I happened to notice
that your books became friendly with mine.
I didn't think that was possible.

But you didn't know
you would have to give up your interests, your camera,
your nutritional habits, salt in potatoes, sugar in coffee,
to become something like a woman, something that
would amaze those who knew you before.
To become a lark from an owl: you will convert to another
    faith.

Poetry is what you want to whisper as you drown,
a dream written out during an exam for which you haven't
    studied.
You've lost so many manuscripts and books,
books you haven't understood, despite having read them
    two or three times.
You used to cry, talk to doctors.
You cuddled with me, hoping to get sick with my soul.

Poems, which I lost,
books which I so frightfully didn't understand,
suddenly bloomed within me all at once,
swarming, pitiless, making my whole body
shake with convulsions, needing to eat and drink,
if only someone would pity me.

You were my confessional, my shelf
for a worn-out book.
You were pages for my words,
ink for my pen,

what there is of poetry.

In the Swimming Pool

They would allow me in 'the frog pond' at Palanga,
in order to teach me how to swim.

The teacher was strict:
you had to do 'the little star' right away,
to swim with boards,
then dive to the bottom
to find the key.

I had no sense of how
I was doing there, on the water.
Much later, during my studies,
I was writing a paper on a phrase
found in Camus' notebooks:
I must write in the same way
that I must swim: because my body
requires it.

My body in adolescence
was ready enough to swim
to suit the lake's initiative.

My daughter's body,
swimming free without repression,
would not pass muster in the kiddie pool.

The lakes of books I swam across
as if drowning – each time I gasped
more dramatically
when I reached the shore.

My daughter's lettering, pressed
all over my documents, is almost
unwilled, resistant to doctrine,
training, and the coach's whistle.

In the swimming pool,
we wave our separate flippers—
just one body and blood
in our sacramental chalice.

Halés Market

All markets have their crazy people—
skulking about, buried under bags,
mumbling under their breath, yet
not so quietly that we do not hear.

Krasavitsa, he says to me, 'beauty':
and it's as if he stuck a finger
in my eye.

There are so many of them here,
so particular, all their own.

In line for chicken,
I hear a cheeping sound—
I glance around: maybe a canary
from the souvenir aisle, or sparrows
in the rafters who have come in from outside;
but no, it's just some chicks
suddenly hatched from their eggs.

The songs of sellers, their smart retorts—
the sign of the cross for a doubtful old lady:
By the love of God, I'm not cheating you!

Clothes offered in two tonal styles—
blackish grey or variegated bright:
you can mark the wearer's aesthetic class.

Astonishing, bludgeoning kitsch:
schizo content festooned with fluff and sparkles,
figurines of newlyweds set beside the crucified.
I believe that Szymborska resides
in a similar paradise.

A good feeling: this vitality of vegetables, the scars
on the backs of carp, the smokey smell of bacon,
intertwining shawls, a piebald pile of tights,
pyjamas with Mickey Mouse, comic strip suspenders.
Yes, I feel good in this wacky abundance of things,
among these cheap impressions for a poem.

I didn't know so much of anything in this life
would astonish me anymore.

Teddy Bear Stuck in a Fence

A photograph on social media—
a fat plush toy by the Sluškų manor,
stuck in the bars on Kosciuškos street,
in the archway's fence to Kalnų Park.
Piles of yellow leaves,
autumn's end.

Perhaps some protesting greenpeacers jailed it,
or maybe it's an installation against Putin's regime.

I rode to save that bear, despite my daughter's chickenpox;
though I never had feelings for such nonsense before—
I never liked stuffed toys, collecting dust;
nevertheless, this one will have its history.

As if we have nothing else to do,
as if war were not hanging over our heads.

By the theatre academy, where I used to go for drama club,
there, where in childhood I played with other girls—
probably some artist's hidden camera is filming me,
or so I thought, as I pulled the toy from out the bars.

It didn't want to go without a fight, and foam was left
scattered on the ground from a wound under its arm.

When the drama teacher was late to our club meeting
(sometimes she never came at all), we'd slip into the hall
    full of props
and strange decorations, costumes of all kinds, back-stage
    knick-knacks.
We'd turn on the blue and red stage lights
and play at acting in a play,
improvising with our meagre creative minds.

'What are you doing here?', sternly asked a man,
probably a director, entering the hall while we performed
something akin to Othello and Desdemona.

'We're putting on a play', we answered
with stunning insolence.

Kids from a television show, corrupted
by a grand, inflated lexicon: talent, and such.

Why take this bear from the bars?
So that I could – when I need to—
strangle it.

Learning to Sew

These threads are so like the line of a road—
I was four, my mum was taking me to town, where,
it could be, she was hoping to meet
my father wandering the streets.

Such hope, on the other hand, made me sick—
and I vomited in the bus.

Those same threads – she sat me in front to see,
and all the way I sewed the invisible stitch
of the highway's centre-line.

Old clothes in the attic;
re-stitching this or that, there would be enough
to last until life's end.

Clearly, there's no sense in that,
unless for ecological considerations.

The textures which touched our bodies,
sometimes dead ones; the lines of the road
mark the Braun attachment zigzags
controlled by an unremembered hand.

That's why I need to learn to sew once more—
to not be sick, to cover myself
in old draperies like a knight
with the armour of stories.

Tremble, you windmills of insanity,
I'm riding stitches
armed with the spears of needles.

are you starting a business? – asked
the store's sewing consultant

no, I'm starting to create

Collecting Colorado Beetles

People have been living here for almost a century.
There is no information for what was here before.
I don't even want to know.

Still, it's so peaceful; I crush Colorado larvae with my fingers,
meditating on potato blossoms and the hooting of trains.
I probably have potato genes – I don't whimper about living
    under turf,
my Spartan upbringing in this place doesn't bother me,
and I remain unsurprised by people's scorn.

Our family albums are plain, nothing in them to shock:
a bad breed generally, maybe even containing crime,
scattered to who knows where, threads broken a hundred
    years back.

I'm speaking abstractly; particular cases are so impressive
that there's nothing you can say; but, generally – banality
    reigns.

People in the photos tried to get by;
they learned how to be safe, proper, and resolute.

Daughters were sewn identical, elegant dresses;
to give them culture – subscriptions to the East German press.

My grandfather, sick with dementia, still speaks about work
    every day;
winter evenings brought suffering, powerless to do anything,
he just sat and crossed his arms.

At home, medals with the ribbons of St. George,
salutations from Putin – on Victory Day,
for the last of the veterans.

I will not scatter ashes on my head;
I hate people who talk themselves into noble origins.

Everyone here is deeply into gardening,
understanding themselves metonymically.

Even I, the loser of the family, trying to buy vegetables
that I don't even need.

People talk about food while at the dinner table;
there simply aren't any other themes.

The only estimable moment in the context of the photos—
it's said my great grandfather who went to drill toilet holes
for livestock wagons

came home and cried.

Kęstutis Navakas is a poet, essayist, literary critic and translator. His poetry has been translated into Russian, Latvian, Georgian, Finnish, Swedish, Macedonian, German and English. Navakas has worked in television as a book reviewer, and been an active promoter of literary and cultural events in his hometown of Kaunas where, in 1996, he opened his own bookshop. He has won prizes including the 2006 National Culture and Art Prize, 2009 Book of the Year and the 2014 Poetry Spring Prize.

the ninth

really really you never need
to doubt that. scientists have
looked into the causes though
they never explained them fully. still
there are people for whom nothing
ever hurt. someone has seen
them. there is evidence to the
contrary that's hard to dismiss:
those people created their own alphabet
discovered the wheel. that means
they can endure they're talented and
Vermeer would paint them. of course

there are such people: their bones are
not buried deep. in the holocene shale

the sixteenth

all the books should be re-written
the words changing places re-arranged
so that books would become incomprehensible
comprehensible books are tiring. the thought
that it is possible to read them only once
is dreadful. if words were water they would
continuously change places on their own
merging into one another after some time
upon opening a book you would find
another text. that's how the book survives.
you can experience it again. each reader
would experience it differently. one book

would be many. if words would mix up take
a look. like water after a cutter has passed.

the sixtieth

a giant star will fall into my lap—
wrote Else, and into my lap will fall
the perfectly chiselled edges of coins

all the epitaphs of the world's gravestones
will stand there: it's strange that we'll
be able to read them in any language at all

gravestones translate their phrases
into any tongue. they don't translate names
the most incomprehensible parts of people

: a fallen coin will one day cut me from what i cannot
    comprehend

the eighty-seventh

standing by the station smoking
newspapers we were more new than
people passing in a comfortable coupe

we were temporary like those
who were left at home we
had coins in our pockets they

grew damp from the sweat of our
palms and the trains went by they
never stop or they stop only for

the minute we can never apprehend

continental

the keyboard of the continental typewriter
is like trampled grass on which Charlie Chaplin
once wrote scripts for silent films in which
everyone always falls the people who played
parts in those scenes are now dead. how strange
it is that we die. how strange that things live on
after us so that we are weaker than things than
citations of some fine phrase we once said which
will also live on after us and the people who heard
and repeated it too. no one will repeat us we are
one of a kind like dead languages nevertheless
we are the true rulers of the world there was only
one ruler of all at a time except for this typewriter
with trampled keys which ruled the world
for more than a century and Charlie Chaplin
wrote on it then someone sometime wrote something
later sometime someone wrote nothing then the scenes
changed more than once until my eyes rolled
along the rusty continental keyboard similar to
trampled grass and finally i felt i'm looking at
the consequences knowing the cause is something else

song

i was speaking. i said it all. i was speaking to the
flies in the room to the tea cup that i just bought
for someone i was speaking to people long dead
about whom i have read i was speaking to my girl and
to the wall of my room. but only the wall replied. but.
the dishes didn't break the clock didn't slip its gears i
managed to pull my palms back in time from the falling
blows of the north wind. and the wall said to me: what's wrong
with you. it's not worth it. if it comes – it comes, said the wall
and if it goes – it goes. what's wrong with you. it reminded me
of books i had read in childhood but someone was actually
eating the smoked fish i hadn't tasted yet but i'm not
seven anymore and everything is how it is for me.
it could be otherwise but i wouldn't want it otherwise.
i was speaking to the wall a good conversationalist i
was speaking with my girl she didn't answer i was
speaking with the clock with my hands with my furniture
and as soon as i heard a shepherd's song (about which i had
only read) wafting from some fields i knew i
understood at once why that song makes me feel so good.

neighbour

a plane flew by destination unknown the people
in flight wearing such colourful clothing they
will disembark at distant airports and their
wonder will be full of joy. the plane has passed
the clouds are heavy and the rain will not end soon
nevertheless, the tulips will bloom in the garden
within a week it will be beautiful maybe
my friends will come by maybe i will write
something on a piece of paper that huddles in fright
maybe i won't need to lock the doors again
the air is heavy and vaguely full of anthracite but
the street overflows with pedestrians carrying colourful
umbrellas and two children run by returning
from school to where a savoury lunch awaits
and maybe some cute domestic pets as well
the clouds hang heavy. the plane has passed.
metal shavings fill the air. my dead neighbour
is being carried from his house. a suicide.
i used to lend him money for the holidays.

lamp

the lamp burns. some birds beyond the window.
somewhere. the sea. books to the left. a forest
to the right. a key in the lock. no one went
anywhere. such silence. this pencil line.
a man lies prone. the lamp burns. the clock ticks.
this pencil line. birds beyond the window.
there is no window. birds beyond the pencil line.
a man lies prone. the lamp burns. glue seeps
into a sealed envelope. a forest to the right. the lamp
burns. the books burn. left. a man lies prone.
his index finger burns. dawn outside. birds
outside. there is no outside. a man lies prone.
his hands burn. the clock ticks. the forest
burns. a man lies prone. beyond the pencil
line. next to the left and next to the right.
the lamp burns. the key burns. elbows burn.
the clock burns. the birds burn beyond
the window. the pencil line melts. leave.

Latvia

Translated by Ieva Lešinska and Jayde Will

Anna Auziņa is a poet, copywriter, reviewer and painter, actively involved in the art world and in art criticism. She has written four well-received, prize-winning collections of poetry and her poems have been translated into several languages, including Russian, German, French and Swedish. Auziņa is the recipient of the Klāvs Elsbergs Prize, the Ojārs Vācietis's Prize and the Diena Culture Award.

Hole

At times I have the overwhelming feeling that love
flows at me in parallel streams—
it is just like at Venta Falls or in the shower
or as if I stood under a huge colander—
and you, my sweet ones,
your eyes, hands, and mouths were holes.

You are the holes when you are happy
to see me, for example,
when mum calls and says that she'll give me
some chocolate to eat on the way,
when someone has come to meet me or has fried some
    squash or made soup,
when my husband handles me gently as if his own flesh,
and at an exhibition the artist comes out
and gives me a hug.

And then there is also that light.
To awaken in a room filled with bright sun
and see the ornaments move on the curtains,
and the day is all clean and young,
you walk out and get dizzy from all that space,
and you are overwhelmed with the need to weep in gratitude,
drop down to your knees in the sand by the sea or in snow,
or in colourful leaves, and say, enraptured:
I wish I were a hole.

And even when my time lacks its honey and ease,
when songs go silent and plant shadows no longer dance
    upon waking,
when mum no longer has soup,
and I have to fry tons of squash all by myself
and help to lift my ailing dad,
without ruining the catheter bag,

and when I myself am that artist
who must hug each visitor
as the only one,

when children make me bigger
and fall out of me one by one as if from a peapod
and all want chocolate and hugs;
when my husband turns away silent
and friends enjoy themselves far off on the beach,
but no, when they are sad and don't turn to me for solace,
when the dog in the country insistently nudges me with
    his nose,
but I have just run out of mash,
when the Riga neighbour no longer brings me a carnation
    on the 8th of March,
because he is unable to leave his flat,
when I no longer get dizzy from too much emotion—
no matter, I will want to be a hole.

I want to be a colander hole—
even if slightly tarnished,
even if only for a tiny, narrow rivulet.

And perhaps it is because I don't know where dad is now
and if it is from where the children came,
and frankly, I am afraid
that we will not rise again in the flesh
yet I cannot imagine anything else that would do;
and even if the ground is not such
that I'd feel like dropping down to my knees,
I can simply nod and conclude drily—
I want it still.

I want to be a hole for love.

IL

I evangelise inebriated

oh my, what am I saying here, friends,
I cannot preach this inebriated—
although, come to think of it, any moment will do

what do you think—
have I never stuffed myself on Good Friday?
I have also spent all vigil dancing at a bar
shaking my hair, stomping my feet,
and that's hardly all I have done

but as, when young, we dropped wherever
when, as adults,
we go to sleep sad in the evening politely
it's okay to whisper: it is bigger than you are

so what are you trying to tell me here
as the night is once again warm and the city is drinking—
don't you know that there is a little puddle in each of us
connected by a rivulet to the sea?
we can also say – with a stem
each branch contains nine blossoms
so functional, the metaphors

so we have been gathered in a bundle
or rather, that's where we originate,
we who were plankton and mountain goats,
all of us who received consciousness
in which He then turned it inside out—
the evolution scheme, like a sock,
and it was very painful

and inside us and under us
He pulsates like a sponge,

and we are in Him like underwater vegetation
and when you walk down the street
every bum has a puddle inside
that will join yours in a common pool
each schoolmate in the old class
every old woman in the parish choir
every Macedonian bastard
and all whom I really don't like
and it really can make it easier
when you try to inhale peacefully when falling asleep

I do like it most of all that we got our consciousness—
for a kitten, I guess, will be absorbed in Him straight
whereas we, as we are going to sleep, can think
how a skating-rink is made on the lake
how robots are getting rid of construction waste
how we rake away autumn leaves
but even we don't ever know for sure
how much rock is still there, underneath,

so now I will have done it intoxicated, my friends
but any moment is the right one of course
and after all, when sober,
I never see you.

IL

76

※◆※

I write this to you.
In the shadow of lindens. In golden shame.
Again and again I find the words to tell you.
You are not you. See. And yet. No matter.
Confession.
Again, I write this to you.
But it's important. Rivulets. Streams.
To say what you already know.
Through and inside us, under the lindens.
And still.
In the dusky confessional. A lamp in the kitchen at night.
Me in a checkered dress. You with unshaven cheeks.
Again and again. It must be said. And again.
Your husband on the other side of the wall. The cool light
    from the screen.
She is not she.
But. I write this. To you.
The paper has yellowed. When I make my peace with it.
When feelings no longer matter.
And yet. The confession itself.
To you, in you, through us. The eyes are at fault.
You, with the pantyhose slipping. Me with unshaven cheeks.
Fitful breath.
In the shade. Again and again.
Floodgate.
I want to say it to you.

IL

Somewhere out in the pasture there is a nest with eggs.
Somewhere under last year's leaves there are stout shoots,
and somewhere there is the back into which they'll grow.
Somewhere out of sight it's clear what's happening.

Somewhere in the forest a beat-up woman draws her last breath.
Somewhere in an old book there are ten roubles between
   the pages.
Somewhere in the attic the she-cat has hidden new offspring.
Somewhere on a yellow note it says that there's salad in
   the fridge.
Somewhere in the pasture truth sways on a bush.

And we can sing all kinds of songs,
we can say that it's wrong to let our imaginations run wild,
and we can imagine again and again,
yet somewhere someone knows precisely
the moment when two cells merged in the oviduct
and the place where the stolen fabric unravels,
and the provenance of the money kept in the book,
and what happens to the love left in a meal.

We can tell all kinds of stories
and put on all kinds of clothing,
we can draw moustaches on our gods,
yet somewhere out in the pasture there is a nest with eggs,
and somewhere someone knows the truth.

IL

Circle

Dad woke me,
he rang in late afternoon
to tell me that
my mum had just died;
I said that I was on my way,
but for a moment I remained still,
trying to figure out
what was wrong here
till I realised that Dad
had been dead for several years,
that it's probably night-time
and mum was luckily fine
and it was she who was calling
to complain that my son
had yet to come home
although the concert was
long since over;

I woke up very young,
for a moment I remained still
till I realised: I'm ashamed
on this dewy autumn morning,
and this shoulder isn't yours,
I have yet to meet you,
and, logically, we have no son,
for he is still in the distant light;
I can sleep a while longer,
till there's another insistent ring,
but this time I am another,
and it is Grandma who rings
so early, before I get up for work,
to greet me on the day of gays
and send her love for Baiba,

I almost believed it,
but then I awoke six years old,
with glasses and a piglet's face,
they were sending me away,
but I threw a tantrum,
till I awoke very old
on a bench in some park,
but a woman sitting nearby
looked familiar,
I sat down next to her
and saw: she is pregnant,
I asked what our plans were
and how it went at the rehearsal,
and generally how she was doing
until I found myself in the maternity ward
and in the most savage of pain,

I thought: never again,
but then we ran down the street,
for they were chasing you;
we had to find shelter right away,
except this time you were another,
one who couldn't lie,
we ran into the past,
but the flat had been broken into;
then I was little on a ship,
my parents had disappeared,
I stumbled and fell on the rails,
perhaps I was drunk,
and then I kneeled on peas to pray,
for you to come back,
but I woke up in a bright classroom,
your daughter at the blackboard
and me as her teacher,
there was a shrill ring for both of us;
I woke up at home again,

Dad was calling again,
although he's been dead for several years,
and then my son rang,
asking when I'll be there,
I made clumsy excuses,
I said: I can't get out,
I'm afraid I'll be late.

IL

now they live on the edge of the city by the railroad
beyond there's only the prison, cemetery, and water tower
it's always damp in the old brick building
even in mid-summer they press together in sleep
if only he's able to get to bed
when awake they wrap themselves in winter clothes

on a Sunday afternoon she can't stand it anymore
and entices him to go out
on the street where hot vibrating light greets them
light full of molecules of linden blossoms, pavement and urine
hand in hand they walk toward the city centre
to have a cup of coffee in a normal café
and even treat themselves to a croissant if she's been paid

and she believes he will no longer be a drunkard
if he washes his hair and puts on a fresh-pressed shirt

and I am her when I hope that the stiff doll will awaken
and expect the round eyes to open translucent

and I am him when I tumble into the warm glop
and brick walls circle around me
and lindens and railway stations

IL

A child grew in me and cancer grew in you.
A child in me – everyone knew about that;
the cancer in you – no one knew.

The child grew quickly, but the cancer grew slowly.
The child was running out of space in me.

Mother undid all the knots in the house,
so that the child could come out of me with ease.

The child pushed against my insides
and broke out of me,
you took it in your arms and rocked it happily.

Cancer remained inside of you and secretly
stealthily continued itself,
until you began to run out of space.

Mother rushed to cover the mirrors,
so you could get out of yourself without fear.

Cancer grew bigger than you,
so everyone knew about it that morning.

My child grew bigger than me
and trudged heavily behind the coffin.

IL

For thirty-eight years I had ants in my pants, I played with fire and stepped on rakes. Now I am taking your country clothes to the fire, I hug your overcoat, I smell your jumper, I crumple your old beret – how we used to mock it, how we begged you not to wear it in the heat of summer, how we tried to make you dress lighter.

There is a special rake for the bonfire; it has well-spaced, sturdy tines. How it annoyed me that you were telling the same story again. And how we watched stars and coals. You always guarded the bonfire, you stayed up until it died down until you finally said – now it's your turn.

Today I say to the overcoat – love, today I say to the beret – forgive me, I kiss it and give it to the fire. Snot down the rake handle.

IL

Uldis Bērziņš is a prolific figure in Latvian literature. Born in Riga, he studied philology at the University of Latvia before studying in Leningrad, Moscow, Uzbekistan, Iceland, Czechoslovakia and Sweden. Bērziņš published his first collection of poetry in 1980 and his poetry has been translated into German, Swedish, Estonian and Lithuanian. He has translated poems from many languages, and has worked on various translations on a grand scale, including the most recent translation into Latvian of both the Bible and the Qur'an. In 2017 he received the Lifetime Achievement Award at the Annual Latvian Literature Awards ceremony.

What was in the very beginning I do not know and will never know. But one thing is for sure and has been confirmed by reliable testimonies. The boy that was me began with his first loud scream: it was my announcement to this war-ravaged land where, fearful and perplexed, the white and purple lilacs of 1944 were about to burst open.

The primeval sound, the brazen conspiracy of throat and tongue against the cannonade there, beyond the forests and bogs. The labial enclosed yowl whose so-called phonetic base, the wondrous interaction between teeth and tongue is still far away... in the future? – in your future, if only you are lucky enough to stay alive in several fateful situations await-ing everyone, awaiting, in fact, any wartime child. The first individual 'chord' from the Indo-European, Ural-Altaic and Semitic morphology. The groundwork for the world that another boy has to now begin to build from ancestral and tribal genes. Groundwork, the very basis for you to be able to say, once you have grown a little, as thousands upon thousands have said before you: in the beginning there was the Word.

IL

It's me here. It's you, it's him.
The forgotten one shows up to ask: where
is that blade of grass reddened with my blood?
I had a bow and arrow, my aim was very narrow
to shoot a bird in a tree. And then I met my maker,
no bird was on his knee. Substance crumbles,
space expands, a cold, misty draught (could that be
Father breathing?), and nothing can be seen
through glass, no matter how semantic,
no one to carry messages to coming ages,
numbers senseless, colours black and what
they taught in school, the Devil takes it back,
no, nonsense. It's me. It's
you, it's him.

IL

John the Moor

Come with elephants from Indus, with horse
herds come from China, bring a horde, Saladin is
laying siege, bridge after bridge, castle after
castle falls, oh prêtre Jean, hurry from the east or
west, ford the Nile, Euphrates and Tigris, Saladin
is laying siege. Why so long, Prester John?
    I will die without seeing Christ's tomb, just to
hold Acre, oh, just hold Acre, hurry, save the
cross that's on my mantle, why so long? In sha'a-llah,
you will make it, Prester John.
    New York, it's nineteen-sixty-something. He
walks into a Lettish store. For the first time since
his mother died. '*Jāni, sveiks!*[1] Why so long?' He
picks up a book from Riga. So tiny in his long blue fingers.

2006, Istanbul

IL

---

1 'Jāni, sveiks!' - Latvian for 'Hello, Jānis!'

The goat! Where Devil fears to tread, there
she is sent – o, goat!
Oh, ah, how steep the paths,
her hooves ascratch,
her short tail moving as she prophesies.
Her beard as noble as her lord's,
nonstop she nibbles with an ardent mouth.
The goat has gnawed away the words,
forbidding us to spend the night! I know
so many folk that would be glad
to stone us,
but now they're out of luck.

2008

IL

Island. After Czeslaw Milosz

Poetry was a telescope: to bring people closer or, for example,
   numbers.
Dear ones! Now I myself have come. Everywhere!
Old age is beautiful, only – why is everything so terribly close?
I open the window, I look at the ocean. Again! Who would
   have thought that darkness would seem too bright?
From Polish poetry, I am left with just 'tak' and 'nie' and
   'dlaczego?'[2]. In other words, I am looking again through a
   telescope – from the fat end.
How tiny are letters in books. And also in magazines, above
   the showcase.
No one left in my loins to make a covenant with God.

2011, Kopavogur

IL

---

2 'tak', 'nie', 'dlaczego' - Polish for 'yes', 'no', 'why'

Odessa. Freudist Motif

'On a summer's night. A quiet summer's night.'

Yes, you became a sailor to bring your mother a nylon coat.
Or: so you wouldn't have to stare at your father's white
teeth, his self-satisfied, smiling mug – oh, sure, smooth,
without wrinkles!

Just to whisk the pennant from coast to coast – oh, your
childhood warrants that as surely as to make slips with the
shrink.

Life came from the sea, and the collective subconscious is
calling it back – or it's the genetic memory as they call it
now.

The ocean is a chamber pot for the rivers to piss in.

2012, Ventspils

IL

Riga Possessive

like a spry dog on a leash, like a billy-goat with beard, the
    devil walks
me Riga-round
on just one naked
word; was kissing here for hours with Zita and with Ita
    from the other
class
I did not care for others;
tout Riga talks like that and now my turn has come to find
    the word
this sentence has to go, hey
Riga's naked speech, your tongue of blushing rose! Although
    I sleep with you,
I do not know your name.

IL

Banished To Time

Like in that Russian movie with boys travelling in time,
there are those damaged frames with a distant moving car
and wires up on poles, yet boys are playing well – young
pioneer cell (oh! a tiny sail at sea! ...) I'm sitting by the fire
and interviewing Thee, but Thou don't answer me. Yet
Thou are inside me! I've had but just one dream in which
Thou weren't inside me. I stood up on a languid shore,
washed by a Mesozoic sea: alone! banished out to Time,
my heart was drowning and eras seemed like seas, time
stepped across the skyline, I will not see Thee anymore,
I'm banished out to Time, I sit before the waves: to talk to
Zodiac who hasn't banished Satan or fair Eve to Time?

Ah! There are no languages. There is no grain, no twin-ear
here! Barren lies the shore: God will be born in me.

2006, Istanbul

IL

Katrīna Rudzīte is a poet and student of anthropology. Her debut collection, *Blur of the Sun* earned her the Annual Latvian Literature Award in 2015. Her poems, critiques and opinion pieces have been published in *Satori*, the literary magazine *Karogs*, and many other publications. Rudzīte has been involved in the prestigious Young Authors Seminar and Prose Workshops led by the Writers' Union and Literary Academy, and was a participant in the 2017 international poetry translation workshop in Riga.

in reality you should have been born a fish
a grey flounder with shiny sides
or a frivolous screech fish
giving itself up to the all-healing voices of the water
which chops the screams off at the root
scattering the bubbles of light in place of the pain

language will rob you of your last strength
transform everything you thought you knew
a beastly language
will wash away the flesh from your bones
mix up your thoughts into a jumbled mess
which you while you swallow dust and fail to breathe
will untangle and squeeze into words

language will tear you into pieces
while you're still alive and warm

don't resist
you are just a message my dear

JW

she has handy portable wings
which she keeps in the drawer
next to her rubber gloves and scissors
each morning she gets up and turns on background noise –
    a massive centrifuge
which while spinning chokes the acid eating up the patches
    of darkness
war and weakness fear kisses
and riled-up Indians travel without abate
through open grey ducts
through a kitchen that's always a little draughty

as the sadness builds
you have to increase the rotations of sounds
until it's no longer possible to hear
the kettle's hissing and millimetres of light tumbling back

JW

when will this poem end?

those winters where you could fall if you weren't careful enough
as ghosts once again play a tune
with transparent tender fingers
leave a dark soot-smeared word under the pillow
like a forgotten scarf
which is later put on the highest shelf

but in the morning
the clouds all the lost memories
unfold into rolling waves of light

and I am no longer that girl
with her hair blowing in the wind with sobs pressed into my
    pillow
with small beasts she sneaks up behind
in silent parks and silent streets hiding in shadows thrown by
    the trees
I no longer swim that way now like a chance foray through
    another's watercolour
with fists made in tenderness and pain

  JW

a person is like an old house on the inside
with rot dust and tattered lost time stuck
on it that you can trip over
while stepping inattentively
there is coal and small red berries dumped into piles
under the beams covered with sobs right before you sleep

a person is quiet on the inside
locked in a dark closet in the hallway
with the nightmares and evil spirits
with the witch with the round face
which always appear in their dreams in the background of a
   dark sea
on the inside a person is soft like a giant cotton ball
dangerous like a poisonous meadow of Apollinaire
and unreasonably far
like a wayward and barely visible constellation

JW

I once read a book how
supposedly every person has someone in their life
who has inexplicable power over them
if one day that person would leave you a message
and offer you to abandon everything and run away
you would do it without thinking
leave your job maybe even delete yourself from social media
suddenly pack your suitcase taking only the most important
   things
clothes a comb and some tool with no clear practical use
for instance an oil painting with a small yellow elephant

sometimes I wonder whether I am also
that person for someone
who they don't really know
but imagines
a lightly rustling treetop in the pit of their stomach
someone they eagerly dream of
while swinging through an endlessly serpentine traffic jam
in the lift after a monotonous work day
or in other stages of reality when it seems that
it's only possible to continue
by opening up a safety net under you invisible to others

JW

a person wraps themselves in colourful scarves
like a bird of paradise
subsists on white flour and seems
they could fly away at any moment
you don't have such strong ties at all with the land and blood
just with trees – it's like they belong only to you
as if you would have planted them in parks and roadsides
where we (normal people) are afraid to tread
after the last bus has driven off

in a kingdom of greasy words and goblins life starts after sunset
in the miserly light of matches you turn into what you would
    have become
if someone had not removed your warm and fragile inner
    cosmos
replacing it with a landscape locked inside a stone cage

JW

The eclipse of language

like a syllable stuck at the dark foot of the heart
I learn to communicate with language
I gain new words and figurative senses
so it wouldn't be so lonely
so language wouldn't want to suck out the blood or create
unnecessary destruction on the nearby playground

I pass the time
as if language was an elderly woman
whose mind is slowly fading
I know quite well how those who have lived in protracted pain
tend to become evil you need to take care of them
like a dog or anxious poltergeist
watch a film with them read to them
bring them bread and coffee from the shop offer to change
    their tired
light bulbs put different shades of green plants
on the windowsills cover the furniture with a soft flower
    pattern
lower your voice while talking
cut their nails when they get angry keep a safe distance
put on a space suit
don't let them touch you or eat from their plates

an eclipse is contagious
an eclipse is brought on by fear
an eclipse can be breathed in or absorbed through the skin

JW

✖✖✖

a green and black darkness
(the kind you experience if you get lost in a thicket by chance)
with precise strokes applied inside him
he gets up already exhausted
his thoughts are as heavy as a piano
which should have been brought up to the second floor last
    spring
sweat dripping through the mattress of the bed
and uneven floorboards
runs under the ground
where condemned literary protagonists
look after the dead
smooth back unruly locks
and lay out the seed potatoes in pretty rows
but you need to live it's always like that as if
nothing happened
as if each new day would touch the skin
light as water

JW

Māris Salējs is a poet, critic and translator, translating from Polish, Ukrainian and Russian. He has worked as a librarian at the University of Latvia and the Academy of Culture in Riga, and contributed to various publications as an author and editor. He was first published in 1994, and his first collection, *Mommy I Saw a Song* came out in 1999, with his second, award-winning collection, following in 2001. A prolific critic and reviewer, Salējs is also the author of many research papers and lengthy analyses of prominent Latvian poets.

✕✕✕

The end of August. The world stops expanding, coils into shape and begins to ripen.

I can no longer walk to the end of the road. Reality has crumbled there. Foliage with all the June birds and nests have been sucked into the hole of the clear-cut. Fog, webbing across the field, catches onto a person who can no longer be distinguished from an apple-tree.
It means: go to the empty universe and, using your memory remnants, revive the velvety thicket and the black lace of foliage against the frozen, inky clouds.
Hornets fly, the last balls of warmth.

A dog barks at a wound in the shape of a cloud.

At nine o'clock, I demand a voice
but I am given a scent.

IL

I can't delve into all that
I can't end and begin in that
I may have to pay for all that
with my life and myself. I lift my hand for a fruit

so transparent it scares me

so I pick up the fruit that's fallen
so I pick up the fruit that's fallen

and let it go up into the tree

IL

neither yours nor mine neither branched nor moved to
another place nor pounced upon me growling
barking. it balls up

into a point in twilight

another one has been paid to stay

IL

✕✕✕

slightly more than me
is needed

slightly more than you
there is

maybe we will go
unnoticed

maybe we will stay
unheard

in the sonorous
great flood

as we wade through city
streets

and the fading day's
dark blood

IL

your last blood flows through the sinews of time smiling
  frostily glassily happily

colourful we are colourful. when we are black-and-white we
  will fall coallike snowlike

on your road

*
so that the last stars can kick us around

IL

It is exquisite being, to swing on the edge of nonbeing
and to not give in to the desire to step over the edge
when the voice approaches the end. when grass grows on
   the lips
and existence squeezes into a thin line
(stabbed out by the sun) come look at me:

I am drinking the sky from a puddle

IL

of course I do not matter and nor do you
all wisdom falls off my lips unsaid
and all that's achieved melts away from the incomplete
oh to touch the uncaptured form of the nonexistent
it walks down in the ravine full of autumn leaves
and rustles like a chance with a deer's gentle nose

IL

The earth has hired me to be its scream. So I try to scream
something green and branched in a tree.

I change colours pop sweat out on my forehead rush into a
red nervation. No glimmer

Millenia have passed I am no longer there trees are free
from me my head is empty
cold takes over my forehead. It's just that tiny person that
walks round with my name

dressed in red or black
his hand out of the glove
he catches the cold's burning sting
while walking on ash scattered
in the snow

IL

Arvis Viguls is a poet, literary critic and translator. He works with English, Spanish, Russian, and Serbo-Croatian languages, and has translated works by authors including Brodsky, Lorca, Whitman and Yeats. Viguls is the author of two well-received poetry collections - *The Room* and *5:00,* and his poems have been published in anthologies and literary magazines in several languages.

At the Dentist's

The metal instruments shine on the tray
like a memory of a nightmare.

Gloves on his hands, a mask over his mouth
and he becomes a faceless executor,
an expert on pain.

His needle cheats pain through pain,
but the drill is not sure of it
and does everything so it is sure.

The lamp for the interrogation is right in my face
 so that I would confess – the flesh is weak,
it feels.

I spit out blood as a reply.
It is all I dare to say.

My mouth is bound
by a dental impression tray.

Afterwards he carefully records it
in my file.

'I made that
tooth as good as new,'
he says
with the smile of a satisfied creator,
who has already taken off his ritual adornments.

I left without looking back,
hoping to never return.

But time and sugar will have its way,
I will be too weak
and one day I will come crawling back,
calling for mercy, begging,
for his sterile metal
to free me from my pain.

JW

At the Hairdresser's

'Very short,' I reply.

'This much,' she shows me,
taking a tuft of it in her fleshy fingers.

'Won't you regret it later?' she becomes curious.

I've also had longer hair.
At the time the hairdresser
had to hold back her tears while cutting it.
No, today I won't regret anything.
Today it's payback time.

Back then my hair
was long like the swing of a blade,
Now I wanted it short
like snipped green shrieks of grass,
short like a pulse.

In those days my hair smelled like the forest,
today I want
it to smell
like sawdust.

There's only two of us in the hair salon,
which suddenly becomes bigger.

The room expands.

I sit silently
in the centre of her cares.
I won't say a word anymore.
I pay her
for this silence as well.

I think
whether my wife would become jealous
if she saw
how this unknown woman
is working around my hair
with her scissors and comb,
running her fingers through my hair,
softly moaning from her efforts,
so she could move her body around the chair.

While she works with her razor
I feel her breath on my neck
this professional with a faint moustache
and the figure of a market meat-seller.
Despite all her efforts,
I am only meat to her.
a sheep being sheared,
a client.

Having reached the end,
she will blow away the fine, black sparks with a hairdryer
from my forehead, nose, ears.

But, as she rubs gel in my hair,
for a brief moment it seems to me
that I am her boy—
an infant in a blue cape,
that she finally undoes and shakes,
shattering this momentary illusion.

'A totally different person!'
she says, proud of what she's done.

Yes I am totally different—
similar to someone,
whose heavy crown is raised from his head
and now he must walk
the cold, rainy streets—
sans sceptre or umbrella,
free, equal and a nobody
like everyone else.

JW

At a Fast Food Restaurant

A girl with a backpack, in the shape of a bear,
despises time.

As if time
were like a roller coaster,
which pulls her forward,
and she has to labour with all her might,
so she doesn't start screaming
and covering her eyes with her hands.

She doesn't try to hurry
with the Happy Meal her father bought her—
a burger and fries,
those forbidden treasures,
scattered in front of her
all golden and enticing.

Their smell alone
would fill her mother with horror,
who counts kilogrammes,
like they count bodies after a catastrophe,
and tries the latest diet
to be more attractive to her new boyfriend
who jeers at her daughter
behind her back.

And she doesn't suck the last
of her pop loudly through the straw
so her father doesn't get annoyed,
who comes to visit her once a month,
so he can fulfill his duties
with an hour or two.

But what does it help,
if soon after he says
that it's time to take her home,
looking anxiously at the three narrow arrows
on his wristwatch—
his holy trinity—
God the Father, God the Son
and the Holy Spirit,
among which there is no place
for a daughter.

JW

Scenes from a Juvenile Detention Centre

With the back of his head towards the camera.

He says that he wants to return to his life.
After this. When this is all over.
When he will have got used to
his own face again.

A view of their sleeping quarters.
Bunk beds.
It could be barracks or a dormitory.
If the keys on the keyring didn't jingle
louder than the siren of the police van.

And at night the lights are turned off
so they can learn to see
their own rage.

Lights out. They're sleeping,
they've put their slippers next to the bed—
a stone put in each one
so they don't fly off anywhere.

But this all remains off-screen.

Meanwhile we have already returned
to our comfortable, well-ordered lives,
where a door means an exit
and they don't have faces.

JW

Brother

You were four when they told you
'This is your brother.'
They didn't explain anything more,
they simply said:
'This is your brother.'

You were curious
and gradually suspicion was born in you.

I followed your footsteps,
everywhere I went you were already in front of me.
The door handle was still warm
as I grasped it in my palm.

And who always sat
in the front seat of the car next to dad—
at the right hand of our father?

You hid me.
Everyone was supposed to think that you're the only one.
How could anyone believe in your powers,
if there's this double
behind your back?

You were afraid that I'd take away your scent
and no one would recognise you anymore.

I stood behind your back
in your old sweater,
my shoes, the laces of which
always came untied.
I stood behind your back

putting stones in my pockets
so the world would finally feel
my weight.

I observed and I studied
I was not yet ready
And I alone developed my abilities
polishing each vertebra,
each joint
that I acquired, standing in the shadows
and waiting,
until you
would not need them anymore.

The sawdust spilled on the ground.
I worked like a patient artisan
while putting myself together.
Sometimes you wanted to drive those stubborn sprouts
right back into me,
the ones, mimicking you,
that mocked you.
You thought they were weapons
which threatened you.

'You can't do that,' they told you
'That's your brother.'
But you didn't believe them.
Being a brother was a task
that I still needed to fulfill.

And I waited.
I observed and I studied.
On the tips of my toes,
I strove to look over your shoulder.

The years worked to my advantage,
And then, one day, I came into the light.

I had acquired the family scent
and I carried the family traits on my face.
The sun was shining, but that didn't bother me.
I finally had a shadow, still I had to break it in.
I was not yet perfect, still I was myself.

'This is my brother,' you said,
'This is my brother.'

JW

Washing Father

He scrubs his father's back.
His father doesn't understand anything
and doesn't reply when others
call his name.

He is too deep
in his body's wrinkles and folds,
too deep for him
to come out of.

Once he awoke in an unknown place.
He put on his glasses.
The lenses steamed up
from what he saw
and his nose began to bleed.

When he returned,
he refused to talk,
forgetting everything
that he had acquired over the years.

His windpipe froze over,
and the circulating blood is still
fighting in vain
to thaw it.

His heartbeats—
they are tracks in the snow
beyond the polar circle.
The wind erases them.

Only the wrinkles
on his skin
are deep – deep
like surgical scars.

Time has left gashes all over his body
like an unskilled surgeon,
who couldn't save anyone,
but just cut and cut, and cut.

He doesn't talk.
His hair grows,
his nails grow,
but he doesn't understand anything.

With a rough towel
he dries his father's body—
a soft towel is of no use to anyone,
a soft towel doesn't absorb moisture.

When he shaves his father's beard,
his father sits in front of him, just
like old times, as he sat in front of
the mirror while shaving himself.

He puts on his father's suitcoat.
It seems too big.
His father shrinks
a few sizes a year.

The suitcoat's pockets are empty
like his father's memory,
its buttons are as dull
as his father's gaze.

He combs his father's hair
and ties his shoes.
He places his father
where the man of the house sits – at the end of the table.

His father doesn't understand anything,
his dominion an arid field,
and he – his son – humbly nurses
that withering legacy of his.

JW

They

They will wash their hands before lunch,
after which the waiter will take away their plates and the
napkins they've used—
dirty and wistful.

His shirt is well-ironed,
and his belt sits comfortably on his waist
sure and trustworthy—
he is buckled in well in his life.

She uses potent perfumes with powerful names—
Passion, *Desire*, *Sin*,
yet always washes her hands in innocence,
and her face is a stranger—
smooth, there is nothing in it that sticks in your mind.

It's only the eye shadows that keep it in this world.

When they return home,
perhaps only lust will make their well-shaped and cared-for
    features ache
like a cramp makes an athlete's foot ache while running.

But their caresses will be business-like,
it will almost be like a transaction.

Then she will get up from bed, wash off her make-up,
they will take a shower separately,
and each will brush their teeth separately,
with only their spit mingling in the same sink drain.

In that bathroom the sink's drain never gets clogged,
in that apartment the plumbing is new,
in that house the pipes are sturdy,
in that neighbourhood the sewage system is faultless,
in that city the water purification facilities are modern,
reliable, and effective like everything,
that brought them together
in this city,
in this neighbourhood,
in this building,
in this apartment,
on this bed
like a pair of legs,
the knees of which never touch.

JW

That Girl,

whom everyone looks back at on the street,
whom everyone wants to buy drinks for at the bar,
whom other women see and pull their men closer to their side—
black flames tattooed on her back above her waist,
a sparkly ring, a shiny lure dangles in her naked navel—
and it's all for nothing,
because that girl will be in despair,
that girl will be alone,
no one will love that girl.

Do you hear me? Sweetie, no one loves tits and asses,
no one loves the bikini line.
No one recognises your brand of perfume,
bloodhounds are already shaving their heads,
readying for the next hunt,
and all that they smell
is fresh meat.

For them you are only
a honey pie in the last row of the cinema,
a sweetheart in the backseat of a car,
a darling in a nightclub toilet for a quickie,
a poster that mechanics put up on the wall in a garage,
so they have something to feast their eyes upon,
before they go home
to their gray, makeup-less wives,
whom they haven't made love to for months,
whom they have fought with to bitter tears,
but who they love unfailingly.

Because we, the fat and bony,
the overweight and bags of bones,
girls with small breasts and big butts,
the pimple-faced, the sweaty,

whose hair is always greasy,
who can't find clothes that fit them—
we are those, whom are truly loved.

Because real love is blind, dear,
real love wears rose-coloured glasses.

Do you see how they look at each other, holding hands,
look how juicily they snog
this girl flat as a board
that guy with tits of fat!
Love has to run through them with supersonic speed,
so they wouldn't care about all of that.

True loves turns a blind eye, sweetie,
but they – all of those men—
they look at you with the eye of a surgeon,
they caress you in the way they caress their touchscreens,
they hold their hand on your knee
in the way they hold their hand on the stick shift in their
   blaring cars.

Beauty will save the world, sweetie,
but before that beauty will be nailed to the cross
again and again, and again
for our sins, the ugly, the imperfect, the unkept—
for the pimples and dandruff,
for the tyres around the stomach and gaps between the teeth,
for the cellulite and bald spots,
for the unshaven bow-legged that are flat-footed,
that stand on the scale every morning
like they're on the edge of a knife.

JW

Inese Zandere is a poet, writer and editor-in-chief of the Liels un mazs publishing company. She has worked as a compiler, editor, and scriptwriter for several newspapers, magazines, publishing houses, and film studios. Zandere has written more than thirty books for children and young people and, over the last twenty years, has been actively involved in projects related to children's literature and cultural education. Her poems, fairy tales, plays, and scripts have inspired the creation of several animation films, theatre plays, and operas for children

in bird sleep

your sleep is surrender
in a battle with the birds
who are trying to turn you into a bird
and force you to speak their bird language
to cry and dig the bed for the daugava
to fly high above the parish orphans on an early November
    morning
so that one of your little white feathers
might fall

onto their first ice

birds administer justice and write laws and observe people's
    nests
when death looks in the window
she has a titmouse's eye
frozen linden walking stick bacon on bony lips
loose shroud of garden gothic comedy
laugh if you're human
laugh softly in your sleep

birds don't know how to laugh

but you breathe peacefully
not noticing
how birds push their beaks into your open mouth
feeding your soul
which will have to fly thousands of kilometres with them
leaving the body here
in this fragile bird sleep

in sleep
where you are so careful and gentle
as if you were afraid to break
your egg   *IL*

radio voices

there are these girls
liega ieva or rita
with short human names and clear radio voices
at night sound carries
as they speak on the radio they don't cry on the radio
on the radio, even girls don't cry
let alone boys
with blue grey brown and green eyes
little radio amateurs always use sensitive mikes
that pick up the rustling sea
and read jokes to the gulls

gulls who laugh out loud

it's late
our listeners are dozing
feverish with the political flu
don't be afraid inese our day will come
just sweat it out now
alert
in the polished panel a watchful green eye
professor eco turns the round knobs
on a semiotic apparatus
finding riga and marvellous foreign sounds
ss šs ts žs ŋš
articulate wind
a pebble thrown into waves
next station *tirana tërhéqës*

night slowly turns to morning
the news rises
hundreds of sleepy arms reach for the radio
and in dawn's light
leave leaning lindens lifeboats lips
leaflets
from which at night
all sibilants were read clean

the girls take off their headphones
pull their shoes to the shore
hang out
nets glasses and ashtrays

but I still hear

rock me radio waves
this is a literary broadcast
I stand at the seashore with ieva and rita with liega
and mirdza bendrupe
listen
to her bright voice on the sibilant sea radio

… a holy bird flew above their shrill clamour with eyes
light green…
magnificently gentle…

IL

Shoe

I lie naked
buried in my dress
dress wind sand
outside metaphors
someone's got my tongue
telling lies with it
quick vibrations that the mouth throws into warm summer air
round bombs
explode silently before reaching the ear
I lie by the sea
my body — my eternal home
a feeling conch shell between coloured cardboard covers
once opened
there's nothing to read
algae and bits of amber
the murmuring conscience of the sea
tosses about a capsized shoe
someone's got my soul
living with it

IL

our bread who art in heaven

I miss you bread

your mouth torn open by the fire
on which you intentionally fell
so that you would be kissed
I miss the sweaty exhaustion
for which your scent is enough
like a blanket over my head
like sleep through the night till the morning

I miss you implacable bread
I miss you like a removed slice
I
flesh of your rye flesh
every flour cell burst
every yeasty eye
sliced open in the cruel film—

I close my own eyes
not to see how it hurts you
bread
it hurts me
bread
bread the knife is between us
sweet hunger always remains between us
and the table
is empty and wide like an outstanding debt

I'm a trampled crumb under the table
I'm a broken slandering tongue
that speaks and withers
and exhausted it slowly emits
the pleasant poison of your taste
without your crust bread

my freedom
is just balled up soft pulp
memory is a clogged cavity in a tooth
destiny is a sparrow's glance
before it carries in its beak up to the heavens
a crumb stolen from earth

let the madness of knives and birds come over us
for theirs is the future, the power, and the void
which is all that will reach you
heavenly bread
give me this day my daily death
that alone
give me this day—

to lie in the belly of the loaf
like a grain that's never been born
press my knees to empty mouth
and fall asleep
in the black bread of my country

IL

137

autumn

the pond is full of leaves and days
I'd like to be a Russian
something forgotten between the floorboards
a little drop
of something unfathomably large

but I'm an exhausted Latvian
so large a part
of something small

IL

attack on the city

black dreadnoughts of nouns
diving from the simmering stream
emerge from the unpassable past
a roar and rumble are heard

raising a charge of waves and a whirl of air
moving the direct stems
dividing conditions on either side of red-hot cannons
firing monosyllabic stone bullets
into the mutely radiant distance of the future perfect

a hail of crystal shudders in the abandoned throne room
lifeboats draw up dripping lexical entries
the translators on the bridge are binoculars in our windows
unsinkable giants of materiality
transforming stanzas bending iron and sound
they will translate this city of ours
back into a single
volcanically stinking word

IL

summer in the country

a flight
in afternoon sleep
with a green airship above a shimmering river highway
where entering a different lane
shiny fish overtake the current

hot bubbles
the courage of a torn petal
along with July
above the sunken city
hanging suspended in wind

losing altitude
sacks of sand poured out in mid-river
long, serpentine grave mounds
shallow shoals of a sad dream

where with six bent pistons
air kicks fallen into water
a winged locomotive
with protruding eyes of faceted mirror
and knives of grey stems in webs cut apart

a straight awakening
on the shortest distance between a heron's neck and a
  sewage pipe

IL

my hands are so cold
that I could warm them with ice
the three wishes are hidden
out of fear
that they might come true
breath held back for so long
it emerges not as steam
but as silver
I don't have to choose any longer
I can be all at once
beautiful happy and smart

IL

Estonia

✕✕✕●✕✕✕

Translated by Adam Cullen & Jayde Will

Kai Aareleid is a novelist, poet and translator and has also written articles, literary reviews and a play. She made her literary debut in 2011 with the publication of her novel, *Russian Blood,* which was nominated for Estonia's most prestigious award for prose. In 2015 she published two poetry collections, *Women on their Way* and *Rain and Wine*. In 2016, she was named Estonian Writer of the Year.

Read me

I
read me
like a poem
read without haste
pronounce each syllable
feel every word on your tongue
weigh the heaviness of each part
of speech
and try to reach the core
you want to

understanding
is possible in many ways
punctuation
marks
can be scattered here and there
writing can be solid or separate
quite randomly
the final meanings
will become clear only later

read me
at your own speed
at my speed
invent new reading positions
play with exclamatory words
onomatopoetry
echoes and pauses
read me

II
read me
like a miniature
I know
it can be a bit one-sided
and will be over too soon
still
read

III
read me
like a novella
it might not be
that much longer
but it has layers
that can be peeled off
like clothes
in a hot room

and there is dimness
halftones
silence
read
me

IV
read me
like a novel
one with two hundred and fifty pages
for those are the best
longer ones have too many words
and those that are shorter
break the borders of genre
although in the end

the shorter the better
in that we concur

read me
like a novel
that has lots of small chapters
that is light and airy
for some things can be left out
of the story
or shaped into a new
novel
of a different taste
and some stories
may remain unwritten
or unfinished

one doesn't always have to reach the end
sometimes there simply isn't enough time
as if you don't already know
read me

V
read me like an epic
but rather your
or my
national epic
let's leave the Anglo-Saxon
and the old Germanic epics aside
these battlegrounds are too wide
and far
and as for the Greeks
I would rather have a
heroine epic
where the woman conquers
the lands and the seas

and the man resists
the hordes of suitors, suitresses
that would be fun

furthermore the hexameter
isn't as natural in our languages
in mine it somehow stumbles
on its six feet
like a limping spider
in your mouth it's simply funny
your mouth
is made for different
songs

and initial rhyme is for both of us
surely the best
that we made clear
at the very beginning
thus
read me like an epic
the first and the last chapter
the summary
the contents
and something from in-between
even if you don't comprehend everything
the sound is still beautiful
old and eternal
read me

VI
read me like a haiku
crisp and crystal-clear
you feel the taste
at once
experts say

that my language would require
a different division
of syllables

well
never mind the syllables
metrics
Kama Sutra
do we even need them

my haiku
is like those Persian
miniature paintings
that grow
beyond their borders

make me
grow
beyond my borders
read me

VII
and write me
for in fact
I'm just a title
and even that might
change along the way
write me

VIII
read me
in your two tongues
and write me anew
in both

IX
finally
read me
like a watermark
that can only be seen against the light
that remains on your iris
read me

AC

Horizon

there are people
born beyond the horizon
in Bukhara or Samarkand

by a boundless yellow
grey rocky
sea of sand
blooming in spring

where the camel caravans of the silk road
arrived from beyond the horizon
and disappeared behind the horizon

there are people
born in the hills of Lisbon
on the edge of Europe
by the last sea

to which the Phoenicians the Carthaginians the Vikings
once arrived on ships
from there beyond the horizon
and the forefathers sailed past the horizon
to find a sea route
to India Cipango Katai
because
the silk road was no more

there are people
born by the rivers
by this very same Rio Tejo
whose other bank is hazy here in the estuary
but in Toledo is the narrow Rio Tajo
turbid from worldly and heavenly
battles

just like my *Emajõgi*
just like my Mother-River

there are people
born by a lake
born by a lake and who die by a lake

there are people
who content themselves with
the worlds painted by others
in order to see
and sing
about the seas deserts rivers
the camel caravans ships journeys
past the horizon

there are people
whose horizons
are the words

there are people

AC

Porto, Porto

come and love me
these couple nights
that I gaze at the sky in this city
the barges on the river
and later the ocean

I have come to go
to finally see that fortress
finish a few chapters
and go

you
won't be going anywhere
you were born here
you can't stand this city
this light this sky
people familiar and foreign
but life holds you here
and you aren't young enough anymore
to change anything

come and love me
a foreign woman
I
will quench your thirst for foreign lands
so that you won't have to leave
will give you back a shred of your youth
for a moment
you
will tell me about ships that cast anchor
trees that dig their roots deep
will whisper promises that don't need to be true
harbour cities like this one
have always harboured trade

we both need
a few lies
we both want
to remember something
to forget something
we both want
come and love me

AC

Rain and Wine

he rose early in the morning
opened the double doors
reflectively traced his thumb across her cheek
said nothing
dressed quietly in the entryway
and left

through the doors was a balcony
two chairs
a table
glasses a bottle of wine upon it

she remained lying there
the curtains stirred
southern morning chill flooded the room
made her shiver

the wine glasses on the balcony table
had collected in themselves the night rain
she had collected in herself
a little drop of another

rain could be poured from the glasses
the person remained

AC

Anchor

at least once each summer
we take a trip
to the edge of the world
to the place where land ends

there
the water is saltier
the pebbles more rounded
on the horizon just the horizon
we cannot get any farther
for now

but you yearn
to go there
beyond the skyline
it's in your eyes
you swim even farther
every time

I look at you and think
I am your anchor
should I be lighter
so that you can go farther
or should I perhaps
not be

I lie on the coarse-grained sand
feel the land under my spine
feel the land echo

my home is here
your home is anywhere

AC

At night the roses

grandfather,

yes
but not later
when I was already sharp and clever
or so I thought
and when he
had crooked rheumatic fingers
thicker and thicker glasses
fewer and fewer teeth

not then

but earlier
when I was still seamless
soft and blonde

how then
in bed at night
he'd read grandma her favourite book
and she would listen
though she'd heard it
time and again
and
how he would stand behind her
by the stove
tickle her
and
feed her fresh honeycombs
first her and only then me
and
how he would cut overripe roses from the garden
pluck off the thorns
take them to her nightstand

157

stick one blossom into her hair
and say
you're just as beautiful as back then

at night the roses' scent permeated
I wouldn't sleep
I would wonder:

just as beautiful as back – when?

and
how come they're my grand-mother and grand-father
when
they seem younger than my parents?

at night the roses' scent permeated
I wouldn't sleep

AC

Indrek Hirv was born into a family of artists, and is a poet, translator and graphic artist who has lived in various European cities. Hirv made his debut in 1987 with his first poetry collection entitled *Dream Rage*. In addition to his extensive poetry collections, he has written several plays, essays, art reviews and memoirs.

✖✖✖

All things around me
have something to say

when they remain silent
I become restless.

JW

✖✖✖

my soul went wandering
it chased after a scent
and can't find the way
back home anymore

JW

✕✖✕

The sun's first sharp rays
cast drowsy shadows
behind the trees

JW

Leaves like heavy
eyelids
the light gleams through them

JW

✖✖✖

when we finally
leave this place

I want to take
your woollen nightshirt
and your long legs along

I'd take them
to the next world too

JW

The smell of your skin
the colour of your eyes
your smile

the fruits of this autumn

JW

✕✕✕

you were taken along
the curtain of fog
is opened slightly
and closed

now you live in me—
like a star
you brighten
my darkness

when you search for yourself
in this abandoned city
come back to me
you will find yourself in me

JW

the first light of the morning
thirsting for the day
for the wind and scents
and voices

the first light in my veins
thirsting for you

JW

Veronika Kivisilla is a poet, storyteller and bard. She studied Estonian language and literature at Tallin University and currently works as a project manager at the Estonian Writers' Union. She has written and compiled textbooks, songbooks and dictionaries, edited and translated literature and published three books of poetry, her 2011 debut collection *Dear Calendar*, the 2012 collection *Veronica officinalis* and the 2015 collection *Cantus firmus*. She also performs as a musician and a performance poet.

I'm at home awaiting a god
awaiting at an open window
my own little god
who should be getting home right about now
the rooms are aired out
a simple meal made from not much of anything steams on
    the table
awaiting us
(it's the end of the month and my wallet's
also been effectively aired out)
but I know that
emptiness is often a blessing
and not much is everything

and here comes my tiny god
everything fluttering around him
blissfully and carelessly
coat flaps sneaker laces scarf backpack
unzipped and wide open
he's dragging a stick across fence posts
and they sing
and only a teensy god
knows how to make such music
he steps inside
and look he's got an ice cream cone
garnished with young pine needles
and he says it's because he knows:
it's good when something's not just sweet
but a little tart and bitter, too

and then he speaks to me
about squirrels and jays and robins
and about how he plays a secret game
that I also played

169

back when I was a tiny god:
if you see a woodpecker
it'll be a good day
we tell each other the exact same stories
over and over
and never tire of them
mom tell me again
what it felt like to hold the bullfinch in your palm
when it flew against the kitchen window that one time
and was lying on the ground unconscious

I watch him and I think:
my god has grown
he's tossed his socks in the corner
and, all on his own, is determinedly tugging
slivers out of his big toe with tweezers
but this god doesn't like washing his feet yet
I see that at night when he sleeps
scratched feet sticking out from under the blanket
but that doesn't stop me
from bowing down and kissing those feet
my god curls his toes for a moment when I kiss them
and then sleeps soundly on
while I sit in the beauty of that divine movement
for a long
long
long while

AC

◆◆◆

Tommy...
Hi!

I truly can't say
how long it's been since we last spoke
but you came to mind for the first time in ages
when I was flipping through old photos:
we were kids together
and you—
my first love
the first bee
to buzz and dance around me
hands purposefully on your hips
wings dashingly behind you
while I daydreamed myself as a daisy,
down in that all-too-familiar pre-school crouch
that includes a skirt that's too short
polka-dot panties
and a perfect full squat
(the next time I did a full squat
was twenty years later,
preparing to give birth...
I've got two kids now, by the way—
what about you?)

Hi!
Can Tommy come out and play?
I asked after I'd climbed to the
fifth floor of the next stairwell over,
and the fifth floor was something
far better than my mere third

171

trainers and a windbreaker
shoestrings and zips still undone
down the stairs like a draught
the door and the world were open
we were kids together
and we had the best climbing trees
a really shady chestnut tree
where we could spy on Old Lady Razumova
(even her name on the mailbox sounded ominous)
and Kula-Mula
(I bet he really did eat children)

Tommy
hah – maybe you remember?—
there in the crown of that chestnut tree, you taught me a
    new word
you'd heard some big kids use
Peter, I'm guessing,
who had a spiffy bike and a MacGyver haircut:
türa!
we were just kids
and neither of us knew its meaning
but I believed you when you said
it sounds so dynamite
and it means:
we've got guts!
when we trilled all afternoon
türa türa!
it became like
an incantation or a war cry

we were kids together
and couldn't understand
why our first kiss
that time there behind the jasmine bushes
wasn't just warm and sweet

but suddenly tasted like shame, too
because the others saw us
and LAUGHED

we fled to your apartment then
lying a long time beneath a blanket on the couch
with our first tenderness and shame
that's where your grandma found us
and said it was just wonderful
that we were playing house
your grandma's name was Haldja! an Estonian fairy
and I wished that she were my grandma
so I could call up from outside
gram-ma! gram-ma!
and then search for the coins for ice cream
tossed into the long grass

Tommy
that's it
because I don't even
remember your last name
but we were kids together once
and I was a flower
and you a bee
and maybe we still are
just a tiny bit even now

AC

HAVE A PLEASANT DAY!

the day and the story start on the train again
just as days and stories often do
a group of pre-schoolers was riding into town
and one of the teachers was,
as the job requires,
teaching them incessantly:

WHAT'D I JUST TELL YOU: NO FIDGETING!
NO LAUGHING OVER THERE!
WE DON'T PICK OUR NOSES!
THERE'S NOTHING YOU NEED FROM YOUR
    BACKPACK RIGHT NOW!
ARE YOU LISTENING? WHAT DO YOU THINK
    YOU'RE DOING?
GIVE ME THAT, RIGHT NOW!
HAVE YOU GONE TOTALLY DEAF, HUH?
and then, in an *especially* loud tone:
NO WHISPERING OVER THERE, WE AGREED TO
    BE NICE AND QUIET ON THE TRAIN!

about twenty baby butterflies fluttering in yellow safety vests
should be an exponentially good omen
because yellow butterflies are said to bring
a warm and golden summer
a warm and golden day…

thank you for taking the train
have a pleasant day!
a familiar female voice recording announced upon arrival
and the children gleefully mimicked:
thank you for taking the train
have a pleasant day!
but one boy whose hoodie read
PROBLEM CHILD

abruptly asked:
teacher, what's a pleasant day?

I TOLD YOU TO BE QUIET!
the teacher shot back
and was highly satisfied with her reply
all the things kids ask,
but what a joy it is that *she* knows
the way things are in the world!

WE'RE GETTING OFF HERE!
COME ON! GET MOVING! NO LAGGING BEHIND!
the teacher corralled the children

and they left… and they left…
that boy who had the problematic hoodie and question
and the girl with a pink backpack
that read WILD PRINCESS

yellow baby butterflies
so wild and problematic…
have a pleasant day!
was my inner wish
one day you'll find out
what a pleasant day is
and you'll have the courage to ask!
I promise
truly:
today, tomorrow, your whole lives:
have a pleasant day!

AC

※※※

I speak of the bedroom of fantasies

a fully-rested couple
wake and stretch luxuriously
on an ergonomic mattress in a spacious bed
the tenderness of morning sunlight upon them
no hollows beneath their eyes

they're served coffee and croissants
that do not crumble
for there are no crumbs in this bed

here, children will never
jump the bedsprings flat
and a muddy-pawed pooch leaping up
is out of the question

and the sheets seem to change themselves
and the blanket never bunches up annoyingly
in one end of the duvet cover

and on the immaculate bedspread lies an open book
that no one will ever read

not a fly pesters here
nor do dust bunnies lie low

the couple that sleeps in this bed performs
regular and mutually-satisfying
intercourse
and also recently attended
tantric sex classes together

therefore there's no point in adding
this bed's occupants dream of no affairs
and not a single secret lover will ever
flop down here, heavens no

no one here snores in drunken stupor
and no one longs for old flames
that glow softly and sorely
in the endless pitch-black autumn night

everything works out anxiety-free

this same bedroom
with this sort of bed
is set up as a display model
in a shopping centre

I say 'shopping centre'
and I muse
people acquire lives and dreams here
believing they're had cheaply
even two or more for the price of one
half-off

oh, the mall
so many pilgrims' destination
horizon and paradise
(bedroom paradise
carpet paradise
curtain paradise
health paradise
candy paradise
plastic paradise)
because everything here
is so unworldly appealing and good

and the mall-goers
pass by the bedroom of fantasies
and consider their own bedrooms

as do I
tossing and turning beside me last night
was my feverish son
I didn't actually notice the golden morning first thing
the windows were fogged up
all existence was, too
and dots danced before my eyes
though they also might have been the splatters of
Brilliant Green on the twelve-year-old wallpaper
from the winter when my kids got chickenpox

we stroll past the mall's bedroom of fantasies
listen – the fantasies unravel like long-kept blankets

only one sleeps sweetly blithely
a vagrant in the nook of a hard bench
not thinking not fantasising once
until the security guard shoos him from paradise

and sleep is unfinished and all dreams and fantasies too

and the first frosts have arrived

AC

Too nice a drunk

locking up my bike in front of the store
a babbling drunk approached me
I wanted to withdraw
but he said
listen
you forgot
to pat your steed after the ride
I was startled but obeyed
pat-pat-pat
went my hand on the seat

approval flashed in the drunk's eyes:
listen
you're young and pretty
but don't you go
sitting on the ground
before spring thunder

I had a sweetheart once
Signe
young and pretty too
but y'see she didn't listen
and was ugly and ill afore long

I gazed upon the drunk
grey-stubbled face
missing most of his teeth
(though his words weren't toothless at all)
but his eyes
were long-lashed
handsome blue kind

that drunk had been a little boy once
for whom purses were searched for sweets
people said
what a boy
what eyelashes
like a doll's
his mother's pride and joy

too kind unfortunately
I thought as I patted my bike
before the ride
and spurred it on our way
mounting the saddle once more
and speeding off

but the drunk sat down
on the ground in front of the store
long before
the first spring thunder

AC

✕✕✕

night sparks candles on the chestnut tree
air sings in an imaginary tongue

a gust through the open window is knowledge
that both our irises
blossomed in synchrony
on this night

I suppose I think about you
in an imaginary tongue
for everything thickens around me
forming a single word
I don't yet know
nor dare say aloud

AC

to be awake and still
so early
when day has appeared for us again
a day like driftwood
on the shore of all days
new and old alike

to be stiller than still
and grasp what is tinier than tiny—
that when silence has become and stayed our jewel
you might even hear how
garden snail penetrates dandelion leaves

to be so still
you might notice anemone's grace
blossom from last year's waste
might divine—
no doubt abundance will one day tower
over each ache

to be truly still
so anticipation holier than holy
might elevate us
so the light of old worlds
might shine
and the hope of the new be perceived

(*diminuendo*)

so we might finally realise
there is no final silence:
only a suspending pause

and then a beginning again

(*piano pianissimo*)

to be so awake and still
to believe
every wingbeat affects
and beetle-prayer

(*sotto voce*)

to be still even yet
when the day has just gone
but to pray before sleep:
deliver us
deliver us from empty clamour

AC

But someday a slow time will start

perhaps on a
Friday night following frenetics and frenzy
when I find in my mailbox a ticket
issued for constant speeding
and you know what:
you've got a several-year debt of silence
we'd ask you to pay
at first opportunity
otherwise we may stop restrict
and even permanently shut down

then the morning must dawn at last
when I wake only by daylight
gather the alarm clock's fallen hands
and the sticks from my head
I'll use them to light the wood-burning stove

all is just beginning to bud
I greet titmice tick- to tockteen minutes
then put stews on the stove
set oxtail soup to quiver
until the broth turns gluish from fat
a leg of lamb in the oven for eternity
beans are already soaking

the slowest
dishes
of all

there's time for grinding spices
for waiting while
caraway and cardamom
surrender their deepest secrets

boiling and baking
become a whole day's doing
I no longer acquiesce to
quell my initial appetite
by gobbling
I want to feel every mouthful
reaching my atoms
nourishing and replenishing them
I've got time to chat with plasma

time for healing old pains
not just swiftly silencing them

when I've finally smeared scented lanolin
down to the tips of my toes
so that henceforth all excess
might simply slide away
I can I start a treatise
in praise of slowness:

bodily speed depends on the frame of reference
by which speed itself is measured

AC

Helena Läks studied philosophy and theology before publishing her first poetry collection *Helena läks – Helena went*, a play on her name. In 2012, she co-founded a small, independent publishing house called Elusamus where she continues to edit and publish books. In 2014 she published her second poetry collection *Corrosion Ache*. She has also written a children's book *The Secret Cat Bakery*, texts for theatre, and contributed to most of Estonia's cultural zines and newspapers.

what she's saying when she says she's not like other women

I'm not like other poets
I'm not like other cat owners
I'm not like other readers
I'm not like other lovers
I'm not like other second fiddles
I'm not like other tenants
I'm not like other shoppers
I'm not like other sauna-goers
I'm not like other tourists
I'm not like other bicyclists
I'm not like other clubbers on this dance floor
I'm not like other lotto players
I'm not like other diners
I'm not like other smokers
I'm not like other patients
I'm not like other borrowers
I'm not like the other fifty percent
but I am pretty self-doubting
you try it, too

AC

✕✕✕

here beneath this starless November Hiiumaa
sky I think of you I think
when you're away then there can't be stars in the sky
I've noticed that before, too

men when missing
their sweetheart they want
to pull down all the
stars moon and space junk from the sky
but when a woman loves
she's always just looking for
starry nights

AC

we're like little animals
bodies pressed close and hearts pounding in chests
seeking warmth and waiting for the world's babel to
subside
we're like stones on a beach as the tide rises
we say goodbye
we're like the last rays of a warm autumn
tender and sorrowful with the surroundings
we're like snares around someone we snap shut
our appetite for other bodies
our craving for other appetites
our souls deep in the darkness prepare to turn the other way
it took time to get to us and we've got to take time
and ultimately give ourselves up to it
no one else may
our arms are for other things
could be for sowing and weeding
they could get moist and muddy
dusty seedy and thus stay clean and warm
warmth our life our tissue's tremble
warmth through two bodies warmth in a dulling day
how long how dunno laugh here blush there
come out in the open with little and nice
be a shoulder, elbow cock and pussy too
wait for me and I'll walk dusty roads
muddy ditches sleeping forests then
we'll lie together there in the room the chill
like we're little animals

AC

palm reader (a.k.a.) don't mention it

an old man wearing
a cotton-padded coat
rubber boots
just stopped before me and said he sees my opening
I was offended
bet he means something disgusting the old pervert
my expression made him rush to clarify
no young lady nothing suggestive
I just looked into your eyes and they tell me
you're going to die before I do

I was offended all the same
well a long life to you then old man I snapped back
the geezer beamed
I suppose that's what he'd been longing to hear

AC

inside his eyes there are glaciers melting
that say: we're coming to visit you soon
we roll down the stairs lay lazily in your bed
kiss your cold toes
but we are colder
tranquillity comes from our mouth
colder than us both
shush we know where to go.

inside his eyes are all the drinks
that I have ever knocked over
the happiness rums boredom beers
oh-why-not wines hey-whatcha-doin' brandies
litres of stories I say are forgotten
because it would be too painful to talk about them

those eyes don't allow you to drown in them
they demand eternal faithfulness
you have to live for that

JW

no plot twist

from time to time a small
mangy fox escapes the dismal grip of his home forest
stealthily making its way for a brief leave
in a raggedy fur coat

from the roar of that forest I once
made a home for myself
plucking the moist lush
moss from its rocks
making all the stars of the sky pale
with my eyes full of watery tears
the sky swirling around and around
oh sky
the hazel trees remained around me
with their leaves fluttering in the wind

in the treetops the waving signs of love
were soaked into everything
that had given birth to me unborn
the moist soil took my footprints
so it could get rid of them soon after

drunk on the senselessness of my youth
I wanted to give my soul to the stars as a present
But it didn't get any higher than the tops of the trees
because we people are tied to them
by fine threads

my home is in the grim love
of this world
and you're like a tree with roots the path
of which is unknown to everyone
the branches greedily spread wide you invite me to swing
for nine days

until I air myself out because of cowardice
and call my ills by name:

the fear of time

the fear of timelessness

the desire to find peace

the urge to make noise

JW

now it could get a little better,
you utter
I nod to the teacups in front of us on the table
it could and actually it should already be better
what are we doing wrong
you ask from the cups

after all
normal people
do their work
press buttons
pull levers
carry out orders
there's no greater evil
than that
yes there really isn't

and us too
we are also normal—
yes you are
confirm the cups
it won't get better until you understand
the cup is half-full and half-empty at the same time
your only evil is ignorance
life gets better gradually
occasionally you have to sit and wait
just don't wait for everything
is what the cups
said

JW

virtsu-kuivastu 12.02.10
(for grandpa)

I ride an ice-eater on the head of a shadow to my home island
on the sides ice harbours in front and behind
a little more departure than arrival
I don't know if there are life jackets on the ice-eater
I've never seen them
Though it doesn't make me anxious
the ice-eater can't sink between the harbours
the top of it will stay above the water
which is why I'm here
mostly under the stars
not in the belly of the eater in the shadows
between the chairs and jackets and sandwiches
I'm a little cold
the ice-eater jerks and shakes as well as
a man who whispers guidance into its ear
makes a thoughtful pause
whoever would see me now would understand
that I am arrogant possessed
by shadows the night and the stars

JW

Maarja Pärtna grew up in Eastern Estonia, moving to Tartu in 2005 where she studied English and comparative literature. She published her first poetry collection, *Grassroots* in 2010, and in 2013 won the prestigious Juhan Liiv award for her poem, 'Bent'. She is co-founder of the independent publishing house Elusamus.

The Meeting

the purely coincidental meeting of two people
at that very moment you are standing right at the crossroads
right in the middle of important decisions
without even being aware of it yourself.

several paths at once
right in front of you
many fates, possibilities

one short breath
and the next thirty years of your life
are already decided

but you understand that only later
in hindsight

JW

The Parting

what happened
what's this silence
distrust

why those sharp words
and well-targeted indifference

what are you hiding
what's hidden behind your sentences
underneath that cool exterior
in the hazy depths of the well, the heart

in the shadow of an outward peace
there's a capriciousness boiling over

your foliage is thin
and there's a face visible on the other side
two pale eyes in the window:
I don't recognise you at all anymore.

JW

The Father

one day he simply disappeared
leaving numerous unfulfilled
promises in his wake
along with a bouquet of flowers
he had bought for her.

they bloomed within a couple of days
were then thrown in the rubbish bin
and taken out along with the other waste.

but the memory of him remained
and turned more transparent with each passing year
until it finally became
luminous and clear—

what was, what could have been
what could have been left
unsaid, unbroken.

he could have been
your father, but now
he's just a gap in
a story that that could have
ended up differently

'…but of course
taking all things into consideration, then
maybe that's actually just fine

or perhaps will be
someday.'

JW

The Bachelor

in the morning while reading
a retired bachelor
leafed through his newspaper
while sitting in the sun

it was his first spring sun
which had both an inviting brightness
as well as a burst of tender shyness

life had taught him
that news in the papers comes and goes
but the joy of sitting in the sun
still remains the same

they can bomb cities to the ground
turn entire countries inside out
even reach out to find new worlds

but the joy of sitting in the sun
yes, the joy of sitting in the sun
still remains the same

JW

border zone

this foreign city's
windy and twilit streets
homes which we were scared of
because of their repelling
facades

the people we were scared of
because of their inaccessible
nature

the territories of bodies
forbidden restricted surrounded with
walls the collapse of which we
both craved and feared

in a forbidden sea of bodies
I carry your heart in my breast.

my place is a border and all
of my shelters are merely
temporary.

JW

communal flat

they turned your building
upside down from the cellar to the attic
they turned it on its head from top to bottom
they broke down the door of your home and argued
that it was living space supposedly allocated to them starting now

in rooms without an address
in a country that world maps
don't remember anymore

the footprints of strangers' lives
on exhausted steps of the stairs
the jangling of the cold latch
on the downstairs door the floorboards' faded
colour the plywood chairs with their tired seats
lined up against the walls

in extremely tiny rooms
in a country where an immense history
accommodated strangers with one yardstick
until smoke from the stove began to blow in
the stove's tile wall collapsed the paint
peeled the tile stove plates
became crooked

and no one cared in the least
how you liked to sit here
in the mornings all by yourself
in your home in your kitchen

the smell of freshly ground coffee in your nose
(the smell of coffee ground with a coffee grinder)
a lilac branch in a vase

or its shadow
like a memory left without a body.

JW

the garden

that photo of a singing starling
which was taken in your garden at home
during that last Soviet summer

is unable to say anything
of his ability to imitate
the voices he hears in
his immediate surroundings

the nest
is fastened to the trunk of a cherry tree
you stand under it in a puddle
wearing little blue rubber boots
and you start to slowly realise
that it's not possible to
direct the path of words
in this world

the starling
in a budding crown
imitates a cat among other things;
meanwhile the cat

sits
on the top rung of
the ladder leading to the hayloft – it's impossible to guess
from his look, what he thinks of that
imitating.

it's impossible to guess
from your look, what that kind of future
means for you.

JW

204

tourist visa

it was in July you returned to that old house
in the woods in the middle of a busy
hay harvest period which is why no one noticed it

all that was left of the two green military barracks
were the outer walls of stacked bricks
the outlines of rooms corners and thresholds
even in the grass that had grown tall
they were still recognisable

the hands and feet still remember them – even the asphalt
    roads
had surrendered to the onslaught of grass
as a few solitary patches except for

the ceiling that collapsed together with
what you couldn't give a name to
as a five year-old – but now?

wild blackcurrants and gooseberries
white transparents, antonovkas

the neural pathways of twigs growing through frameless
    windows
through non-existing walls right into the kitchen and
    living room
under an indescribable blue sky

it appeared that they didn't
remember much of anything
from their life as pruned garden plants.

JW

Mats Traat worked as a farm labourer after finishing technical college before studying in Moscow, first at the Literature Institute and later at the Institute of Cinema. He then worked as an editor at the Tallinfilm Film Studio and has been a professional writer since 1970. A prolific poet and novelist, Traat has lived in an independent Estonia, Estonia under Soviet occupation, under Nazi German occupation and Soviet occupation once again. Traat has published over twenty poetry collections and been the recipient of multiple awards, including the 2011 Jaan Kross Literary Award.

An August Evening at Nine o'Clock

A telephone
a candlestick with a question mark
the smell of new and old books
apples

What have I done today then

I went to town went on the metro
I offered a woman my seat
she didn't sit down
She said she's getting off at the next stop
who did she remind me of

Myself only myself

Who was saved on that day
who disappeared
I don't know

I took my medication I talked with my doctor
his telephone was busy for a long time

JW

✕✕✕

A man with a suitcase plods along in the pouring rain,
an otherworldly oddity from another time
in the aggressive current of cars

The proper ones are in tin casings,
tin men, lead soldiers.

The man with the suitcase plods along in the pouring rain,
a rosehip blossom on his chest
against the darkening background of the future.

The proper ones are in tin casings.

JW

A school handicraft lesson

I crease a clean sheet of paper
with my thumbnail.
And I stop perplexed.
Brain folds weather-beaten by the years,
having forgotten, how to make a little ship.

Only my nails grow
unimpeded.

JW

Epicrisis

the surgeons cut out
one piece
after another
out of you

dark urges
prejudices
defiance

one piece
after another
soon you'll be clean

and the voice of light swells
full of good intentions

JW

Breakfast

In a spiritual bind, in the confines of kitsch
I weigh each syllable.

A person measures parameters,
and a dream a person.

Life's path?
Was that the path,
that was travelled along so quickly?

A trail between the cliffs
often on the edge of an abyss.
Clouds threatening overhead,
a raven's *nevermore*.

Life's path?

The mind growing
ever entangled by a
a dreamlike detached clarity.
It's here I am now. I am drinking coffee
in a hotel in Riga's Old Town
on a November morning.
And I think:
Perhaps man is actually
an embankment for life's path?

JW

Room to Live

the sun sinks into the sea
a person into helplessness
unpolished thoughts ownerless odes
strangers' beliefs
on his neck as a life preserver

in order to escape his problems
he puts on rose-coloured glasses
and his head in the ground

unnoticed
a person's concerns are instead taken over
by a fairy
a hobgoblin
an oracle

Crafty Hans Old Devil Frankenstein

a wind turbine
in an absurd time

JW

Special treatment

How far ahead can man rush? His mind feverish, he suddenly
  stops—
the machine contested, ruthless artificial intelligence! At last
  man retreats
to the cellar of the subconscious. A robot drags him out from
  there,
thrusting a goblet of poison upon him: bottoms up, the last
  Socrates!

JW

Vexation

Understanding turned inside out, an overdose of arrogance.
Foreign planes violate borders, evil rumbles below in the
    water.
The world resonates from explosions, there are rivers of
    blood flowing.
The air is full of menace. Humanity is as inert as gas.

What can you grab onto in the middle of the evening, or
    your existence?
Everything, which thought touches, seems slippery,
floating past, but at the same time fixed, heavy.

Light has its own weight and colours, a parallel truth.
Twilight, a spectral analysis would show your colour,
map out your areas, where you erase
your annoying unmanageable presentiments.

Only the weather vane exalts the mind,
affirms faith in a bright tomorrow,
in an indelible sunlight.

JW

About the translators

Rimas Uzgiris is a poet, translator, editor and critic. His work has appeared in *Barrow Street, AGNI, Atlanta Review, Iowa Review, Quiddity, Hudson Review, Vilnius Review* and other journals, and he is translation editor and primary translator of *How the Earth Carries Us: New Lithuanian Poets*. Uzgiris holds a Ph.D. in philosophy from the University of Wisconsin-Madison, and an MFA in creative writing from Rutgers-Newark University. Recipient of a Fulbright Scholar Grant, a National Endowment for the Arts Literature Translation Fellowship, and the Poetry Spring 2016 Award for translations of Lithuanian poetry into other languages, he teaches translation at Vilnius University.

Ieva Lešinska studied English at the University of Riga. From 1978 to 1987 she lived and worked in the USA before moving to Sweden to work as a freelance journalist and translator, while pursuing a Master of Arts in Baltic philology at the University of Stockholm. She currently lives in Riga, where she works as chief translator at the Bank of Latvia, and as a freelance journalist and translator. She has translated the poetry of Seamus Heaney, Robert Frost, D H Lawrence, Ezra Pound, Dylan Thomas, T S Eliot and various American Beat Generation poets into Latvian, and has published numerous English translations of Latvian authors in periodicals and anthologies in the UK and the US.

Adam Cullen is a freelance translator of Estonian prose, poetry and plays into English. Among other authors, he has translated novels by Tõnu Õnnepalu and Mihkel Mutt and poems by Jürgen Rooste, Veronika Kivisilla, and Asko Künnap. His translation of Õnnepalu's *Radio* was nominated for the 2014 Cultural Endowment of Estonia's Prize for Literary Translation from Estonian into a Foreign Language. He is a member of the Estonian Writers' Union and on the board of its Translators Section. Originally from Minnesota, he now lives in Estonia.

Parthian Baltic Poetry

The Rules of Bird Hunting

Eeva Park

Phenomena

Eduards Aivars

Beasts

Krišjānis Zeļģis

Narcoses

Madara Gruntmane

The Moon is a Pill

Aušra Kaziliūnaitė

Now I Understand

Marius Burokas